Ellen M Mitchell

A Study of Greek Philosophy

Ellen M Mitchell
A Study of Greek Philosophy
ISBN/EAN: 9783337078065

Printed in Europe, USA, Canada, Australia, Japan

Cover: Foto ©Thomas Meinert / pixelio.de

More available books at **www.hansebooks.com**

A STUDY OF
GREEK PHILOSOPHY

BY

ELLEN M. MITCHELL.

WITH AN INTRODUCTION

BY WILLIAM ROUNSEVILLE ALGER.

CHICAGO:
S. C. GRIGGS AND COMPANY.
1891.

TO

THE KANT CLUB OF DENVER

THIS VOLUME IS DEDICATED.

PREFACE.

IT may be interesting to my readers to know something of the genesis of this book. Twelve years ago, in St. Louis, a little band of women used to assemble every week to study and discuss the problems of philosophy. I led the circle as teacher and learner. Beginning with the study of Greek thought, and applying myself diligently to the works of its great masters, and the commentaries to be found in English, German and French, I sought continually to make clear to others what became clear to myself. At the end of two years, the circle in St. Louis was exchanged for one in Denver, but with unabated interest and enthusiasm on my own part and that of my co-workers. At their request, the verbal exposition became a written one, and finally developed into its present form. Whatever merit it possesses is due in part to those who have helped me towards the light by their eager questions, their hesitation at the obscure, their quick appreciation of spiritual truth hidden beneath abstruse phraseology, their loving fellowship and sympathy.

Above all other teachers I am indebted to Dr. William T. Harris. From him I first learned to seek philosophy in the history of philosophy, and to find it everywhere as the spiritual interpretation of the universe. I have also received help and stimulus from the expositions and lectures of Prof. F. Louis Soldan, of St. Louis; Prof. D. J. Snider, of Chicago; Prof. Thomas Davidson, of New York; from the Concord School of Philosophy, and the Kant Club, of Denver.

I have consulted all the accessible authorities, but have relied chiefly on the histories of Greek philosophy by Zeller and Hegel. The quotations are from the original German, except where I have availed myself of those of Dr. Harris, in his translation of Hegel's chapters on Plato and Aristotle, published in *The Journal of Speculative Philosophy*. The greater part of Zeller's work is to be found in an English translation, but not that of Hegel, with the above exception.

In order not to encumber my pages with notes and quotation marks, I here acknowledge my general indebtedness to Zeller and Hegel, and append a list of the most important works that I have read and studied in the prosecution of my task.

ELLEN M. MITCHELL.

SYRACUSE, N. Y., August, 1891.

A LIST OF REFERENCE BOOKS ON GREEK PHILOSOPHY.

DIE PHILOSOPHIE DER GRIECHEN, EINE UNTERSUCHUNG UBER CHARACTER, GANG UND HAUPTMOMENTE IHRER ENTWICKELUNG. By Ed. Zeller. English translation of a part of this work by Sarah F. Alleyne, O. J. Reichel, Alfred Goodwin, and Evelyn Abbott.

VORLESUNGEN UBER DIE GESCHICHTE DER PHILOSOPHIE. By G. W. Hegel. English translation of the chapters on Plato and Aristotle by Dr. William T. Harris, in *The Journal of Speculative Philosophy*.

GESCHICHTE DER PHILOSOPHIE IM UMRISS. By Albert Schwegler. Two English translations, the first by J. H. Sterling, the second by J. H. Seelye.

HISTORY OF PHILOSOPHY. From Thales to the Present Time. By Friedrich Ueberweg. English translation by Prof. George S. Morris.

GESCHICHTE DER PHILOSOPHIE. By J. E. Erdmann. English translation, edited by Prof. Williston S. Hough.

INTRODUCTION A L'HISTOIRE DE LA PHILOSOPHIE. By Victor Cousin. English translation, by O. W. Wight.

LECTURES ON GREEK PHILOSOPHY. By James Frederick Ferrier.

ANCIENT AND MODERN PHILOSOPHY. By Frederick Denison Maurice.

CHRISTIANITY AND GREEK PHILOSOPHY. By B. F. Cocker, D. D.

THE SCIENCE OF THOUGHT. By Charles Carroll Everett.

THE FRAGMENTS OF PARMENIDES. Translated by Thomas Davidson, *The Journal of Speculative Philosophy*.

PLATO'S WORKS, translated into German, with Introductions, by F. Schleiermacher.

PLATO'S DIALOGUES. Translated into English, with Analyses, by Prof. B. Jowett.

ARISTOTLE. By Sir Alexander Grant.

ARISTOTLE'S DE ANIMA. English translation, with introduction and notes, by Edwin Wallace.

ARISTOTLE'S ETHICS. English translation, with notes and essays, by Sir Alexander Grant.

ARISTOTLE'S POLITICS. English translation, with notes, by Prof. B. Jowett.

OUTLINES OF THE PHILOSOPHY OF ARISTOTLE. By Edwin Wallace.

ESSAI SUR LA MÉTAPHYSIQUE D'ARISTOTE. By Felix Ravaisson.

PROLEGOMENA TO ETHICS. By Thomas Hill Green.

THE JOURNAL OF SPECULATIVE PHILOSOPHY. Edited by Dr. William T. Harris.

CONTENTS.

INTRODUCTION.

THE CLAIM AND CHARM OF PHILOSOPHY AS A STUDY. By William Rounseville Alger.

Page

CHAPTER I.

PHILOSOPHY AND HISTORY. Philosophy a progressive process of knowledge comprehending the progressive process of culture; philosophy a history of philosophy; self-knowledge and knowledge of the world; philosophy the self-knowledge of the human race. . . . 1

CHAPTER II.

CHARACTER OF GREEK PHILOSOPHY. Greek being the unity of the spiritual and the natural; the stage of Greek consciousness the stage of beauty: the classic style in philosophy; contrast between Greek and modern philosophy. 4

CHAPTER III.

PRE-SOPHISTIC PHILOSOPHY. The rise of philosophy in Greece; perception of nature its basis; the Ionian philosophers, the Pythagoreans, the Eleatics, Heraclitus, the Atomists, Anaxagoras. 7

CHAPTER IV.

THE IONIC PHILOSOPHERS. Thales; his proposition that water is the originative principle of all things an attempt to trace multiplicity back to unity; Anaximander; Anaximenes; the philosophic significance of Ionic philosophy. 10

CHAPTER V.

PYTHAGORAS AND THE PYTHAGOREANS. Fabulous stories of Pythagoras; the Pythagorean Order; Aristotle's explanation of the Pythagorean principle; number both form and substance, but the two not yet definitely separated; mathematics and music; metempsychosis; the Doric character of Pythagoreanism. 14

CHAPTER VI.

THE ELEATICS. Thought freed wholly from the finite affirms its own infinity; Xenophanes declares that God is pure spirit; the principle of Parmenides pure being; the contradiction between Being and Appearance; Zeno the inventor of dialectic; his arguments against the possibility of motion; the importance of the Eleatic principle and its influence upon language. 19

CHAPTER VII.

HERACLITUS. The principle of the Becoming; fire the symbol of the Becoming; the consciousness of truth a consciousness of the universal; the principle of the Becoming antithetical to that of Being, but both alike valid. . 27

CHAPTER VIII.

EMPEDOCLES. A mediator between God and men; doctrine of the four elements; two moving forces, love and hate; belief in metempsychosis; value of his philosophy. 31

CHAPTER IX.

THE ATOMISTS. Leucippus and Democritus; the full and the void, or atoms and empty space; atoms an object of

CONTENTS. xi

thought, not of sensuous experience; the Atomistic philosophy a mediation between the principles of Heraclitus and of the Eleatics. 36

CHAPTER X.

ANAXAGORAS. Athens and Sparta; the principle of Anaxagoras intelligence ($νοῦς$); its mechanical application; individualized atoms; Anaxagoras closes the old period and opens the new. 40

CHAPTER XI.

THE SOPHISTS. Influence of democracy upon philosophy; the true meaning of culture; theoretical and practical egoism; definition of the sophist; method of Greek education; rhetorical skill of the Sophists; their final criterion of judgment "particular subjectivity," the individual self; relativity of truth and goodness; the Sophists the Encyclopædists of Greece. 45

CHAPTER XII.

INDIVIDUAL SOPHISTS. Protagoras; his fundamental proposition, "Man is the measure of all things;" its one-sided interpretation, truth is relative, not absolute; the three propositions of Gorgias; based on the contradictory nature of sensuous phenomena they are unanswerable from that point of view. 55

CHAPTER XIII.

SOCRATES. The teaching of Socrates the positive complement of the Sophistic philosophy; one principle represented at different stages of growth by Socrates, Plato, and Aristotle; the philosophy of Socrates closely connected with his life; his mode of instruction; his character a model of virtue; his friendship for young men; Xanthippe; his inner absorption; different interpretations of his "dæ-

mon," or "genius;" the characteristics of Greek and
modern consciousness united in Socrates. . . . 61

CHAPTER XIV.

THE FATE OF SOCRATES. His trial; his fate the tragedy of Athens and Greece; his last hours: Socrates and
Aristophanes; the teachings of Socrates misunderstood;
Socrates the precursor and founder of our moral view of
the world; the truth of Subjectivity not the exclusive
feeling of self, but the universal *idea* of self. . . 70

CHAPTER XV.

THE SOURCES AND CHARACTERISTICS OF THE
SOCRATIC PHILOSOPHY. The union of the ethical
and the scientific, morality and knowledge; an absolute
moral authority at the basis of self-consciousness; true
knowledge derived from correct concepts; the Socratic
method; the Socratic irony; the Socratic Eros; the Socratic process of induction and definition; the relation
between the universal concepts of Socrates and the Ideas
of Plato. 78

CHAPTER XVI.

THE SOCRATIC ETHICS. Virtue true knowledge; self-
knowledge morally essential; the attainment of moral
independence; the concept of the Good and its abstract
character; the office of friendship; the state, the family,
and the individual; an ideal view of nature; the Socratic
trinity, knowledge, virtue, happiness. 85

CHAPTER XVII.

THE PARTIAL DISCIPLES OF SOCRATES. Varied
character of the impression produced by Socrates; Euclid
and the Megarian School; Antisthenes and the Cynics;
Aristippus and the Cyrenaics; the only complete Socratist
Plato. 92

CHAPTER XVIII.

PLATO'S LIFE AND WRITINGS. Early influences; acquaintance with Socrates; travels; the Academy; personal character; quotation from Goethe; arrangement of his dialogues. 102

CHAPTER XIX.

CHARACTER OF PLATO'S PHILOSOPHY. Socratic basis of Plato's philosophy; idealism the deepest principle of all speculation; form of Plato's exposition; employment of myths; knowledge the activity of the soul itself in the sphere of Ideas; virtue based upon knowledge; exaltation of Love; Dialectic; Idea of the Good; allegory of the cave; meaning of education; philosophy the royal science; quotation from Emerson. 109

CHAPTER XX.

THE PLATONIC DIALECTIC. Dialectic the science of true Being, the inquiry into Ideas; Ideas the eternal prototypes of Being; the laws of thought objective as well as subjective; opinion the middle ground between ignorance and knowledge; knowledge as opposed to perception considered in the Theætetus; the ideas of movement and rest, of Being and non-Being, investigated in the Sophist; Being defined in the Parmenides as a unity which includes multiplicity; the distinction between the absolute and the relative in the Philebus; dialectic inseparably united with moral culture; the Divine reason identified with God. . . 119

CHAPTER XXI.

THE PLATONIC PHYSICS. Views of nature in the Timæus; creation of the world; the world-soul; Hegel's interpretation of Plato's thought; matter; the human soul; the doctrine of reminiscence; immortality; retribution after death; ethics the central point of Platonic philosophy. 137

CHAPTER XXII.

THE PLATONIC ETHICS. The good the endeavor of the soul to become like God; philosophy a means of purification; virtue the internal harmony and health of the soul; virtue its own reward, vice its own punishment; justice the fundamental principle of Plato's ethics; his ideal Republic; his communistic views; violation of subjective freedom; Science of the Beautiful; the basis of Plato's philosophy the substantial Idea; the older Academy.   147

CHAPTER XXIII.

LIFE AND WRITINGS OF ARISTOTLE. Early influences; relation to Plato; tutor of Alexander the Great; school in Athens; technical and popular lectures; style of exposition; stupendous achievements in science and philosophy; strange fate of his manuscripts; Aristotle's writings the basis of Scholasticism; their influence upon modern thinkers. 163

CHAPTER XXIV.

GENERAL CHARACTER OF THE ARISTOTELIAN PHILOSOPHY. Philosophy the knowledge of final causes; Aristotle not an empiricist, but unites scientific observation with dialectic; his style severely logical; the Platonic idea the Aristotelian form toward which the sensuous strives with inner necessity; Aristotle's philosophy original and independent, though resting on a Socratic-Platonic basis. 170

CHAPTER XXV.

ARISTOTLE'S LOGIC. The formal activity of the pure understanding described by Aristotle for all time; the categories; the nature of the concept; the judgment and the syllogism; the theory of scientific demonstration; a necessary limit to mediatory knowing; the "prior in nature" and the "prior for us;" proofs of probability; the laws of the understanding formal laws, to attain speculative truth its logic must become the logic of Reason. . 175

CHAPTER XXVI.

ARISTOTLE'S METAPHYSICS. First Philosophy, or Wisdom; Being-in-itself the common basis of categories and propositions; earlier theories examined and criticized by Aristotle; agreement and disagreement with Plato; the Idea with both related to an objective reality, but Plato emphasizes its transcendence, Aristotle its immanence; the relation of form to matter; the becoming, or the nature of change; the substrate of change matter; matter pure potentiality; motion the energy of matter; motion presupposes a moving cause itself unmoved, Absolute Spirit; the universe a continuous system of ascending progression; Absolute Good the final end of everything; the Divine activity the activity of pure thought; God not mere abstract Being, but living, eternal Energy. . 182

CHAPTER XXVII.

ARISTOTLE'S PHYSICS. Nature as a whole a gradual overcoming of matter through form; motion, space, time; life the power of self-motion; the soul, *entelechy*, the unity which embraces life, sense-perception, and thought; the vegetative, the sensitive, and the cognitive soul; *dunamis* and *energeia*; free-will; the active and the passive reason. 197

CHAPTER XXVIII.

ARISTOTLE'S ETHICS. Happiness the chief good for man; its highest realization participation in the blessed life of God; the moral significance of *dunamis* and *energeia;* natural tendencies the basis of morality, but morality their transformation through rational insight and will; the law of moderation; moral and intellectual virtue; the relation of happiness to self-consciousness; the distinction between happiness and pleasure; the highest virtue an excellence of the intellect; friendship. 210

CHAPTER XXIX.

ARISTOTLE'S POLITICS, PHILOSOPHY OF ART, ETC. Politics the presupposition and completion of ethics; the relation of the family; prejudice against trade and traffic; opposition to Plato's communism; Aristotle's ideal state; his views on education; wise men rather than wise laws; the ultimate identification of politics with ethics; Art closely connected with spiritual development: purification (katharsis); the Peripatetic School. 217

CHAPTER XXX.

TRANSITION TO THE POST-ARISTOTELIAN PHILOSOPHY. The affirmation of self-thinking Reason the culmination of Greek philosophy; thought the unity of the subjective and objective with Aristotle; later schools neglect the objective and emphasize the subjective; abstract universality of thought in Stoicism; abstract individuality of feeling in Epicureanism; the negation of this one-sidedness in Scepticism; the final attempt to solve the dualism between subjective and objective in Neo-Platonism. 225

CHAPTER XXXI.

STOICISM. Life and character of Zeno; aim of Stoic philosophy the exercise of virtue; virtue depends upon knowledge; Stoic view of nature dynamic; Destiny and Providence; the human will identified with universal law through self-conscious obedience; pleasure, not the aim, but a result of moral activity, different from virtue in essence and kind; duty for its own sake a categorical imperative; the ideal wise man; self-culture and the social well-being of the community; a universal human brotherhood. . . , ... 229

CHAPTER XXXII.

EPICUREANISM. Personal influence of Epicurus; the aim of philosophy to promote happiness; theoretical interests subordinated to practical; the test of truth sensuous perception; Epicurus the inventor of empirical physics and empirical psychology; the supreme good not to suffer; virtue never an end in itself, but a means to pleasure; the highest form of social life friendship; one and the same principle viewed from opposite sides in Stoicism and Epicureanism. 245

CHAPTER XXXIII.

SCEPTICISM. Philosophy contains in itself the negative of Scepticism as its own dialectic; the New Academy; the contrast between thought and being; Pyrrho of Elis; the ten tropes; the consciousness of the negative and the definition of its forms of the highest importance in philosophy. 254

CHAPTER XXXIV.

ECLECTICISM. Character of Eclecticism; Cicero the representative Roman Eclectic; the softened Stoicism of Seneca, Epictetus, and Marcus Aurelius; Plutarch's aim in philosophy to create moral character; the union of Hellenic philosophy and Hebraic theology in Philo. . . . 261

CHAPTER XXXV.

NEO-PLATONISM. The aim of Neo-Platonism; Platonism posits the One only as the primitive source of all being; the One produces *nous*, pure reason; pure reason produces the world-soul; the human soul once a part of the world-soul; its descent into the sensuous from which it must be freed to regain its original purity; the perfect life the life of thought; the highest knowledge the self-intuition of reason; mystical union with God the final aim of philosophy; the doctrines of Platonism popularized by

Porphyry; the speculative basis of religion sought by Jamblichus; Proclus the representative of Scholasticism in Greek philosophy; the creation of the finite and its return to the Infinite conceived as a spiral descent and ascent; the ways to God three, love, truth, faith: the altar of the Absolute One a luminous centre in whose flame all is consumed and united; Neo-Platonism a high idealism. 265

CHAPTER XXXVI.

THE CLOSE OF GREEK PHILOSOPHY. The great work achieved by human reason in Greek philosophy; the propædeutic office it fulfilled for Christianity; its affirmation of the existence of God and of the soul; its identification of faith and knowledge, God's revelation to man and man's discovery of God. 279

INTRODUCTION.

THE CLAIM AND CHARM OF PHILOSOPHY AS A STUDY.

THE REASON that so many persons study the less important and less attractive branches of knowledge, while so few turn their attention to its supreme department, is that a multitude perceive the value and the interest of the inferior parts where one appreciates the claim and charm of the all-commanding whole. In the special domains of study the materials lie open to the senses and the understanding, in tangible form, to be experimentally dealt with, and to be mastered by efforts easily made, little by little. But in that universal field of principles, laws and processes, which philosophy covers, the appeal is made to the reflective faculties and speculative insight; and these, with the vast majority of persons, are not keenly alive but undeveloped and disinclined to exertion.

For every student of philosophy, without doubt, there are a hundred students of botany. Aside from utility, there is a strong attraction to the investigation of the structure and life of plants and flowers; for they comprise one of the chief domains of material beauty. But, both in dignity of range and intensity of interest, how incomparably superior is the study of metaphysics; since this explores the very ground and nature and operation of beauty itself, not merely in its physical manifestations but also in its intellectual and moral forms, and in its constituent essence as the living revelation of the perfection of God!

So there are a thousand avid devourers of poetry and romantic literature where there is one earnest reader of philosophical dissertations and treatises. This is because the pictures and narration of the former delight the craving sensuous powers of the mind, and exact no costly effort; while the profound discrimination and sustained stretch of the latter overtask the attention and interest of all except serious and robust spirits. And yet what an immense advantage the ripe philosopher has over the mere poet or romanticist, in the solid service and joy yielded by the exercise of their respective gifts and discipline! For while poetry pleases, with the rich loveliness and freedom of its productions, philosophy, not content with an empty enjoyment of them, lays bare the innermost secrets of those productions, and of their origin, by expounding the fundamental nature and offices of the imagination and rhythm and metaphor, whereby their matter is given and their spells are woven. All other modes of inquisitive spiritual activity are partial and preliminary; philosophy alone final or complete.

The etymological force of the word philosophy is the love of wisdom. Seizing this, we grasp a descriptive phrase, not a definition; we take possession of the practical substance but miss the dialectic essence. Nevertheless this fructiferous ethical aspect is almost as valuable as the constitutive procedure itself. For the keenest metaphysical analysis or synthesis is no more than a vacant gymnastic of abstractions, if it do not begin and end in the love of wisdom. Wisdom is knowledge enriching experience with blessed fruits. Wisdom is assimilative insight in fruition at its goal. And to the pursuit of this man has an integral vocation lodged in the generic core of his being. Luminous demonstration of the accuracy of this statement is easy, and may be given in a single sentence.

As the transcendent paragon of animals, the only one who caps the climax of animality with the surpassing crown of rationality, *man fulfills his destiny* by the progressive attainment of applied and enjoyed truth. And that is the real definition of wisdom. What is wisdom but truth happily realized in a living experience of its uses? All knowledge that falls short of this is mere information in a storehouse. Wisdom is the term or end in which alone a rational nature reposes with satisfaction. Familiarity with it, according to a wonderful passage of Scripture, is friendship with that Divine Playfellow whose delight is in the children of men. Thus understood, is it not obvious that the study of philosophy presents both a claim and a charm of the supreme order?

But let us leave the surface of description, and enter the depth of definition. What is philosophy? It is that form of thinking wherein all the parts imply one another, and every part implies the whole. It is that kind of knowledge which has its presuppositions in itself, and is, therefore, independent of all other knowledge, while all other knowledge is dependent on it. It is the self-seizure of the idea in reflective consciousness. It is the science of self-activity. It is the pure search after the First Principle, the finding of it, and the deduction thence of all else. It takes for its province those elements and methods which are common to all the special sciences, and groups them in a sovereign unification. Hence, with entire justice, it has generally been designated the science of sciences, queen of all the rest.

The definition of philosophy given by the great masters of thinking are all in substantial agreement under their verbal differences. For example, Ueberweg formulates it as the Science of Principles; Fichte, as the Science of Knowledge; Rosmini, as the Science of Ultimate Grounds. In response to every why asked by the human mind the philosopher undertakes to reach an answer so comprehensive and final that it cannot be transcended. The aim of philosophical study, then, is the conquest of truth in its universal essence, aspects, relations, source and end. And so it is the specialty of its royal prerogative to forerun, pervade and follow, all the other sciences which are subdivided under its universality, and subordinated to its authority. Its cultivators study the nature and providence of God, in theology; the character and experience of man, in psychology; the phenomena and laws of the universe, in cosmology; and the varied treasures of the other special domains of knowledge, under their several rubrics. In all these departments the laws of consciousness, observation, cognition, discrimination, classification, congruity, are the same; and they can be furnished by philosophy alone. It is, then, plainly, unrivaled in its importance.

Strenuous efforts have recently been made in several elaborate lectures to show that ethical science does not depend either on religion or philosophy, but is every way competent to itself. This is a shallow confusion of thought, and an unwarrantable use of language. The case may be conclusively stated in a nutshell thus: Philosophy is the science of ultimate grounds. Morality is the science of right and wrong in human conduct. Every concept that enters into it, such as causation, duty, conscience, motive, sanction, vice, crime, penalty, derives its significance from certain principles, theoretical and practical. If moral science furnishes these principles from its own resources, it is itself a philosophy. If it looks elsewhere for them, it presupposes a foundation deeper and broader than itself. By consequence, ethics necessarily rests on philosophy.

There is another consideration which places the importance and the attractiveness of this study in a still more striking light. The highest intellectual power and dignity of which our nature is capable can be realized only through the cultivation of philosophy, which deals directly with the sublimest thoughts conceivable by any minds created or uncreated. Consider, for instance, the content of the idea of absolute perfection indicated by the word God. The meaning of this word, the greatest in human language, is a completely self-determined Person, who is a free infinitude of love, wisdom, power, holiness and bliss, forever giving himself to a boundless number of persons, whom he creates for the purpose of multiplying his perfecfection by them! Such is the developed Christian idea of God. Pure act is a self-distinguishing unity, which has no potentialities. That is, all possible presuppositions are actualized in it. This is at once the realized experience of God and the offered destiny of man. Being is knowableness; and man is a free power of determining it for himself. His determinations of pure being are ideas, which are universal and infinite in their nature. There is nothing real apart from thought; for the thinking of God originates all that is. And thought can comprehend all else while nothing else can comprehend thought. Knowledge, without which ignorance could not be known, is participation of omniscience; as duration, without which time could not be known, is participation of eternity. And knowledge is possible only as the progressive actualization in us of a self-consciousness in itself complete, and in itself including the universe as its object. That is to say, all true knowledge in man is his participation of the creative thinking of God. Thus we become, as the New Testament says, " partakers of the divine nature." What other dignity is worthy of comparison with this? But clearly it cannot be bestowed by any degree of familiarity with the physical sciences, or with the political sciences, or with historic or literary lore. It is to be achieved by the development of the spirit in the study of philosophy.

It is astonishing how materialistic science is overrated and ideal philosophy underrated at the present time. It is as if one should put a high value on a pebble because he can clutch it, and despise a star because he cannot. A popular declaimer, whose name rings through America, says, "Darwin contented himself with giving to his fellowmen the greatest and the sublimest truths that man has spoken since lips uttered speech!" What are those truths? That all through nature there is a struggle for existence, from the lowest vermin to the highest animals; and that in that struggle a law of natural selection causes the survival of those best fitted to their environment. Whatever value may be assigned to these formulas, surely they cannot, for purity, grandeur, beauty, inspiring power, stand in any comparison with the cardinal doctrines of philosophy, such as the perfection of God, the infinity of intellect, the immortality of the soul, the absolute authority of right. The weightiest sentences Darwin ever wrote are utterly insignificant when set along side of any one of hundreds of sentences which may be quoted from the really sovereign thinkers represented by Plato, Aristotle, Augustine, Aquinas, Leibnitz, Kant, Hegel.

No one able to appreciate them can pay even passing attention to such statements as the following, without seeing that the study of philosophy is the sublimest and worthiest of all studies. Infinite being is the object of thought, and personal spirit is the thinking subject capable of distinguishing it into infinite determinations. Being is one and personalities are innumerable: but the whole of the object is for every one of the subjects. Consciousness is a potential infinite; because it cannot be limited by anything of which it is unconscious. Therefore it is exclusively self-limited; and self-limitation is the definition of the true infinite. Consciousness is a self-determinable mirror which becomes whatever it reflects. For certainly nothing can enter consciousness save as this from its own substance creates a representation of that which enters it. Here is matter for one to muse over with worshiping wonder as long as he lives.

Finally, in illustration of the claim and charm of philosophy as a study, we must say that it is not only the most comprehensive and exalted of all studies, but it is also the purest, the freest, the most beautiful and delightful. The subject is self-contained and the student is self-sufficing. Stimulants and aids may be attained abroad, from books and from teachers. But all the essential data are in the student himself. The learning faculties, being, nature, life, humanity, God, are all within his immediate reach, just as they were with Fichte or with Pythagoras. And great attainments were as easy for the ancient masters of insight as they are for the latest student, because all that they did for themselves he must now do for himself in his own psychical work-shop. If the deepest thoughts have been thought many times already it is none the less necessary that each new comer think them again. He never can obtain them from another.

And nothing can be imagined cleaner, lovelier, or more precious, than the task whose triumphant accomplishment initiates the performer, even in this dim world, into that sacred hierarchy of intelligences who contemplate the divine archetypes. The differential and integral calculus is the science of continuous being and its determinations, in the mathematical or formal order. The dialectic is the science of continuous being and its determinations, in the moral or substantial order. Leibnitz began the unification of these two and Swedenborg wished to continue it. When some inspired genius, in the future, shall complete this unification of the mathematical and the metaphysical dialectic, and simplify it for popular communication, the epoch of illumination and redemption for which travailing humanity waits so long will dawn.

In the meantime what matchless privileges wait on the secluded employment of the philosopher! That the study of metaphysics is repulsively dry, barren, knotty and wearisome, is a vulgar prejudice of ignorance and frivolity. Earnestness and patience will find it no more difficult than the other chief disciplines of wisdom. It deals with the ideal realities of good, truth, right, use, beauty, immortality, in their origins and ultimates. And these are the substantial thoughts of God by whose means the thinking subject,—under the lights of nature, reason, and divinity,

—changes itself from natural shadow through rational reflection into divine substance.

This is a province of culture preëminently suitable for women, it is so pure a domain of beauty.

> How charming is divine philosophy!
> Not harsh and crabbed as dull fools suppose;
> But musical as is Apollo's lute,
> And a perpetual feast of nectared sweets
> Where no crude surfeit reigns.

The accomplished and amiable writer of the present work herein sets an excellent example which it is to be hoped a multitude of her sisters will be quick to follow. Nothing can become them better or profit them more. It is an employment without any compromises either of modesty, refinement or aspiration. No perishable tools are needed. No filthy experiments with furnaces and retorts or earths and smuts and moulds and rots are called for. And however arduously the workers toil they make no noise and leave no chips or dust or slag. The material is spirit, the labor is silence, the course is intelligence and affection, the product is wisdom and character, the path of advance is infinity, the goal is God. And if that goal be a retreating one the pursuer carries at every step a substantial reflex of it in his own breast.

WILLIAM ROUNSEVILLE ALGER.

A STUDY OF GREEK PHILOSOPHY.

CHAPTER I.

PHILOSOPHY AND HISTORY.

TO understand what is meant by philosophy we must understand what is meant by development, that it implies not only potentiality but reality. One may say that man is reasonable by nature, but in the child, reason is a possibility not yet realized. Education must develop and bring it to consciousness. Our potentialities as spiritual beings are infinite, but are transformed into realities only through an active coöperation which makes them objects of conscious endeavor and aspiration. As the seed under favorable conditions produces the plant, the blossom, the fruit, and returns again to seed, the spiritual germ in man expands, unfolds, and produces its fruit. But here the comparison ceases, for the spiritual fruit becomes matter for a higher form of growth, a higher grade of development. Each age inherits the culture and experience of preceding ages, and though a particular race or people may retrograde by reason of external conflicts or inner exhaustion, humanity as a whole steadily and consistently develops its latent possibilities. Progress is not in a straight line, but in a series of widening circles. "Philosophy looks through the totality of circles, comprehending in a progressive process of knowledge the progessive process of culture," says Kuno Fischer.

What else, then, is philosophy, except a history of philosophy? Are we to look for reason only in the products of nature, and not in those of spirit? He who considers the different systems of philosophy as mere accidents instead of a necessity, doubts the rule of reason. If the universe is divinely governed, each great system of thought must possess historic worth and historic truth. For the object of knowledge in philosophy is the human spirit itself, and truth is a living process which develops and advances in the civilizing course of humanity.

"But does not philosophy embrace in its problems something more than the human spirit?" asks Kuno Fischer. We call it self-knowledge; it calls itself knowledge of the world. Only a few times in the course of its history has the Delphic word, "Know thyself," appeared at the head of philosophy, as the first of all problems. Whenever this has happened there has come a turning point in its history; as with the Socratic epoch in ancient times, the Kantian in modern times. These epochs would not so clearly illuminate the way on all sides if they did not bring to light the nature of the matter in its whole extent.

Human self-knowledge is not only the deepest but the most comprehensive of all problems, including in itself, if carefully analyzed, knowledge of the world. Does this statement appear incredible? Surely it is not difficult to see that the world as an object of thought is only possible under the condition of a self-conscious being who makes it such an object, such a problem. Here we reach the great riddle of things. What is the world independent of our thought, our representation of it? Is there any knowledge of it distinct from and independent of human self-knowledge? Is not philosophy the self-knowledge attained by the human race in its successive stages of development? Does it not seek to comprehend the innermost motive of every form of culture, to make clear to the human spirit its own strivings?

What lies in the act of self-knowledge applied to our individual consciousness? We draw back from the external world, make the life we have hitherto lived an object of reflection, regard it critically and perceive its defects. Can we return to the old condition? No, we are freed from it in a measure, we are no longer what we were; earnest self-knowledge is a renewal and transformation of our life. It is a crisis, a turning-point in our spiritual career, preparing us for new interests and higher forms of culture than those we have outlived. We begin to philosophize so far as we are able, and our philosophy is a fruit of our culture, however ripe or unripe. This is the significance of self-knowledge in the experience and development of individual life. Similar crises occur in the collected life of humanity, and are expressed in the great systems of philosophy, which work as historic factors in the culture of successive ages, defining and influencing progress, identical on one side with the spirit of their time, but introducing, on the other, a new form of development.

CHAPTER II.

CHARACTER OF GREEK PHILOSOPHY.

ONE people above all was philosophic in antiquity, the Greek. Their philosophy sprang from the basis of their national life, and can only be comprehended by studying the peculiarities of Greek being. They received the beginnings of their religion and their culture from Asia and from Egypt, but so transformed and enriched the foreign material that all which we recognize and value in it is essentially Greek. They breathed into it the breath of spiritual life, the soul of freedom and beauty. They even forgot, ungratefully, the foreign sources of their culture, and looked upon it wholly as their own merit and achievement. Hegel calls the Greek spirit the plastic artist, forming the stone into a work of art. The stone does not remain stone in this formative process, but is transfigured by the idea shining through it: nevertheless, without the stone, the artist could not embody the idea. Herein lies the distinctive character of Greek being, that unbroken unity of the spiritual and the natural, which constitutes at once its glory and its limitation.

Breaking through the Oriental dependence on the powers of nature, the Greek subordinates the sensuous to a tool and sign of the spiritual, and supplants his own natural condition by the higher one of a morally free, beautiful human culture. The happiness he strives for he wishes to attain through the development of his bodily and spiritual powers, through vigorous participation in the thoughts and activities of his fellow-citizens. His morality rests upon the basis of natural disposition. From the old Greek point of view man is not required to renounce his physical desires and be changed in the depths of his being; the natural inclinations as such are justified, virtue consists in the development of every faculty, and the highest moral law is to follow the course of nature freely and reasonably, observing the right measure and proportion. The custom of his people is to the Greek the highest moral authority, life in and for the State the highest duty; beyond these limits he scarcely recognizes moral obligation. This very limitation, the narrowness of Greek relations and sympathies, was fitted to produce great individualities, classic characters.

The stage of Greek consciousness is the stage of beauty. There is no contradiction present between the sensuous appearance and the idea; one completely realizes and interprets the other. Thus the Greeks remain unrivaled masters for all time in sculpture, in the epic, the classic form of architecture. Religion and art are identified. "The Greek divine service," says Mr. Denton J. Snider, "was an act of the poetic imagination; worship was a poem conceived, if not sung; therein was the worshiper elevated into the presence of the beautiful God, into whose image he was to transform himself, and be a living embodiment of the Religion of Beauty."

This plastic spirit characterizes Greek activity even in the domain of philosophy. Nothing is forced or artificial in the development of its problems; nowhere is there a break in the advancing course of ideas; a connection of the most vital kind unites the members of this far-extended series into one harmonious whole. "That plastic quiet with which a Parmenides, a Plato, an Aristotle, treat the most difficult problems," says Zeller, "is the same thing in the domain of scientific thinking that we call the classic style in that of art."

The Greek philosopher directs himself simply to the matter, and accepts what appears to him as true and real. This immediate relation to the object of his thought was only possible because it proceeded from a more imperfect experience, a more limited knowledge of nature, a weaker development of inner life, than our own. The modern philosopher has to deal with a greater mass of facts and laws, facts carefully examined, laws strictly defined. Hence his critical attitude. He begins with doubt, and is forced by his starting-point to keep the possibility and the conditions of knowledge in continual sight.

At the beginning of Greek philosophy, it is the external world which first draws attention to itself, and suggests the question as to its causes. What lies at the basis of all the changes which the senses perceive? What is the substance out of which the world is made? This question is followed by another. How is the world made? These two taken together express the main problem of Greek philosophy: How do matter and form unite? The character of the answers I shall seek to interpret in the following pages.

CHAPTER III.

PRE-SOPHISTIC PHILOSOPHY.

THIS division includes the Ionian philosophers, Thales, Anaximander, and Anaximenes; Pythagoras and his disciples; the Eleatics, Xenophanes, Parmenides, and Zeno; Heraclitus, Empedocles, Leucippus, Democritus, and Anaxagoras.

Greek philosophy began in the sixth century B. C., born in the Ionian colonies of Asia Minor at the time of their political decadence. Crœsus and the Lydians had first imperiled Ionian freedom; later, the Persians destroyed it wholly. Dissatisfied with the world of reality which lay in ruins, thought fled to an ideal realm of its own creation.

Perception of nature is the basis from which this early philosophy proceeds. The universal is conceived in a material form, as water, air, etc. But water as the fundamental element of things, the primitive substance underneath nature's manifold changes, can only be an object of thought, not of sensuous perception. To say that all things are made of water is to say also that these many appearances of nature perceived by the senses proceed from one cause. Multiplicity is traced back to unity; the Many are comprehended in the One.

Thought makes a farther advance when the Pythagoreans conceive the essence of things as number. Without matter there could not be number, since we could have neither extension nor division in space and time. But number itself is immaterial, lifted above the world of the senses, though not independent of it wholly.

The Eleatics go a step farther; abstract their principle from everything material, and call it pure Being. Change is impossible, they say ; how is anything to pass from an unchangeable to a changeable condition ? How did the world begin ? Beginning implies movement ; how could the immovable move ? Fixing their gaze on the unity of thought, they deny the multiplicity of nature, deny nature altogether. They first make the great discovery that contradictions are contained in our natural thinking, that the sensuous representation of the world is not the true one—a discovery rich in results for all time.

Heraclitus regards the problem from another point of view. To him, also, it is incomprehensible that the unchangeable should change. But he does not therefore deny change ; he affirms it as the fact of all facts, and believes that it is eternal, that "everything flows," that the essence of things is itself the Becoming. He makes energy the primal principle instead of the Ionic matter. Becoming is the unity of being and non-being ; something is, and at the same time is not. The whole world of experience is in a state of transition from one condition to another. All finite existences are changing, passing away. Transitoriness belongs to the nature of finite being. Hence the Eleatics denied it, denied the world of matter, and affirmed the reality of the infinite — the world of thought. The principle of Heraclitus implies, on the other hand, the infinite within the finite, as the divine activity producing change.

Empedocles and the Atomists offer another explanation. Matter itself is considered as the abiding, the unchanging. What we call change is produced by the union and separation of numberless primordial elements or atoms.

Anaxagoras took the next step in philosophy. Whence come the order and arrangement of the world, if the atoms are only drawn together by a mechanical, blind movement? What is it that directs the movement? It must be an intelligent principle, says Anaxagoras. The essence of the world is mind, not matter.

Here the first period of Greek philosophy closes. The problems of nature have been so far investigated that from their solutions spirit proceeds as the moving, directing thought—self-creative activity.

CHAPTER IV.

THE IONIC PHILOSOPHERS.

THALES.—With Thales we begin the history of philosophy. He was a native of Miletus, born about 640 B. C., a contemporary of Krœsus and Solon. His position at the head of the Seven Wise Men proves that he was greatly esteemed for practical wisdom by his fellow-citizens. He is supposed to have studied mathematics in Egypt, and was the first to teach geometry in Greece. Diogenes Laertius relates an anecdote illustrating his interest in astronomy. Looking up to observe the stars, he fell into a ditch, and the people mocked him that, seeking to comprehend heavenly things, he could not see what lay at his feet. This is an old version of the common reproach brought against philosophers and philosophy. One critic remarks that the mockers could not stumble and fall into the ditch because they lay there already and never looked upward.

Thales left no writings. All we know of his philosophy is the proposition that all things arise from and consist of water. Aristotle suggests that Thales was led to this thought by observing that dampness belongs to the nature of seeds and nutriment; that warmth itself comes from moisture, and thereby life itself. So far as we know, Thales did little more than enunciate his principle. Wherein, then, lies his philosophic significance?

Why does philosophy begin with Thales? Because he first makes the attempt to explain natural appearances from their universal ground. He draws back from the world of nature, where he sees only change and multiplicity, and seeks to reduce all things to one simple substance, uncreated and imperishable. This substance he calls water, giving it a physical form, but meaning by it the essence of things, that which is not perceived by the senses, the unity underlying multiplicity. It was a grand affirmation of the human spirit, this affirmation of the One made by Thales in that old Greek world where the very gods had a theogony and were many and changing.

Anaximander.—Anaximander of Miletus, some years younger than Thales, appears to have been his friend and disciple. He was the first to apply the word principle (ἀρχή) to the original essence which he assumed. What he meant by this essence which he defined as "unlimited, eternal and unconditioned," is not clear to his commentators. It was neither "water nor air," but "contains in itself and rules everything," and is "divine, immortal, imperishable." The parts of the infinite change, but it is itself unchangeable. It is farther said to be infinite in magnitude, but not in number. Anaximander affirmed its absolute continuity, but not its absolute discretion, as was afterwards maintained by Anaxagoras, Empedocles, and the Atomists. Aristotle is supposed to have been alluding to Anaximander when he speaks of a principle which is neither water nor air, but "thicker than air and thinner than water." It is certainly material, and seems to have been matter generally, since Anaximander separates from it the elemental opposites, warm and cold, moist and dry, and brings together the homogeneous in such a way that what is gold becomes gold, what is earth becomes earth, and yet nothing arises or begins to be, but all is contained potentially in the original substance. This imperfect attempt to trace back natural appearances scientifically and to explain the world from physical grounds denotes a great advance of thought in comparison with the myths of the old cosmogonies.

Anaximenes.—Anaximenes was younger than Anaximander, and is supposed to have been one of his disciples. Like Thales he represents the absolute under a physical form, but as air instead of water. Air seems less material than water; we do not see it, but feel its motion. "As our soul, which is air, holds us together, so spirit and air, which are synonymous, animate the universe." He thus compares his essence to the soul, and seems to form a transition from the natural philosophy of his predecessors to the philosophy of consciousness.

Diogenes of Apollonia, Idæus of Himera, and Archelaus, are also called Ionian philosophers, but we know little of them except their names, and that they supported in part or wholly the views of their predecessors.

Aristotle calls attention to the fact that the earth is not assumed as a first principle by any of these early philosophers, because it appears like an aggregate of many single parts, and does not represent unity in a sensuous form as completely as water, air or fire. The greatness of their thought consisted in their conception of one universal substance, expressed as a form of matter, but uncreated and imperishable, at the basis of nature's changing and manifold appearances.

CHAPTER V.

PYTHAGORAS AND THE PYTHAGOREANS.

THE next step in philosophy was taken by Pythagoras of Samos, who lived between 540 and 500 B. C. He is the hero of many fabulous stories, and the accounts we possess of his life and achievements are so interwoven with the fanciful inventions of his later adherents that we cannot tell what is or is not historical. He is supposed to have traveled in Egypt and through intercourse with its priestly caste to have conceived the idea which he afterwards executed, the foundation of a society or order devoted to man's moral regeneration. Upon his return he settled at Crotona, in Lower Italy, or Magna Græcia, where he appears to have distinguished himself not only as a statesman, a warrior, and a political law-giver, but as a teacher of morality and personal culture. He is said to have possessed great personal beauty and a majestic presence, which, added to his eloquence, inspired his listeners with awe and admiration. He was the first to give himself the name of φιλόσοφος (lover of wisdom), instead of σοφός (the wise man).

He not only instructed his friends but associated them together in a peculiar form of life, which developed into what is known as the Pythagorean order, similar in character to the voluntary monasticism of modern times. Whoever wished to join this order was subjected to a novitiate of five years, during which period he must preserve strict silence. It is claimed by a modern philosopher that it is an essential condition of true culture to receive at first without question the thoughts of others. The members of this order wore a uniform dress of white linen and led a regular life, each hour of the day having its appointed task. It was enjoined upon all that they should reflect night and morning upon the events of the preceding day in order to determine wherein their actions had been right or wrong. They ate in common; their chief food was bread and honey, their only drink water. They abstained from meat on account of their belief in the transmigration of souls. Among vegetables, beans were forbidden as an article of diet, for what reason is not clear.

Notwithstanding its high moral significance in the history of Greek culture and of humanity, it was impossible that an order like this having no connection with the public and religious life of the Greeks should be long maintained. Hence we find no trace of its existence as a formal union of individuals after the death of Pythagoras, which is variously stated as occurring in his eightieth or one hundred and fourth year. That any select number of citizens should distinguish themselves either by a peculiar mode of dress or of life was foreign to the idea of the Greek state, whose members stood on a perfect equality one with the other. Even the priests who guarded the Mysteries did not form a caste as in Egypt, but took an active part in public affairs, and were in no way set apart from their fellow-citizens.

Turning to the Pythagorean system of philosophy we find it to have been the work of different men and times. Its principal thoughts came probably from Pythagoras himself, but history leaves the point uncertain. Aristotle, who is our chief authority in the matter, speaks of the Pythagoreans, never of Pythagoras. The principle they affirmed was number; "number is the essence of all things." How did they reach this thought? Did it spring from their love of law and order in the life of man, leading them to observe the regularity of natural phenomena in the movements of the planets and the relations of tones? Aristotle says that they believed there was greater resemblance in number to that "which is, and happens, than in fire, water, or earth."

But what did they mean? Did they regard numbers as things themselves, or as their archetypes, separated from them as the thoughts of an artist from his work? Aristotle explains their theory in this way; number is both form and substance, but the two are not yet definitely separated in thought. This was an advance beyond the Ionic point of view, from a principle purely sensuous to the abstract relation of quantity. Aristotle quotes Plato as saying that the mathematical attributes of things belong neither to the world of the senses, nor to that of ideas, but mediate between both; different from the sensuous because they are eternal and unchangeable, different from ideas because they contain multiplicity.

Pythagoras applying his philosophic theory to music, argued that although there might be qualitative differences as between men's voices and wind instruments, the peculiar relation of tones to each other upon which harmony depends is a relation of numbers. He also sought to construc mathematically the heavenly bodies of the visible universe. They are represented as ten, which was regarded as the most perfect number: the Milky Way, or the fixed stars; Saturn, Jupiter, Mars, Venus, Mercury, the Sun, the Moon, the Earth, and the Counter-Earth. It is uncertain whether this Counter-Earth meant the opposite side of our planet, or one wholly distinct from it. Aristotle thinks it was invented to complete the number ten. The earth was supposed to revolve around a central fire, which was called the Watch of Zeus. Each heavenly body as it moved produced a different tone, according to its size and speed, and thus arose that harmonious world-chorus, the "music of the spheres," which we do not hear, say the Pythagoreans, because it is identical with our own substance and being.

A similar theory was applied to the soul. It was conceived as a harmony, a counterpart of the heavenly system, dwelling in the body as in a prison. To this was added the belief in metempsychosis, a doctrine stretching far back to India, but borrowed from Egypt by Pythagoras. Pythagoras claimed to possess a distinct recollection of having passed through various stages of existence—as the son of Hermes, and Euphorbus in the Trojan war.

To comprehend Pythagoreanism we must study the

conditions of Greek culture in the sixth century B. C. As a reformatory movement it belongs to that series of ethical strivings which we trace in the works of Epimenides, in the rise of the Mysteries, in the teachings of the Gnomic poets and of the Seven Wise Men. It also bears the stamp of the Doric race character and the Doric institutions. Its aristocratic politics, its music, its gymnastic, its admission of women to the culture and society of men, its severe morality, its regard for the traditional customs and laws, its veneration of the old and of superiors—all were essentially Dorian. But it received from Ionic physiology the impulse towards a scientific explanation of the world. Pythagoras transplanted philosophy from its old Ionic home, in Asia Minor, to Italy, that it might there develop under new conditions.

CHAPTER VI.

THE ELEATICS.

THE Eleatics carried the process begun by the Pythagoreans to its ultimate limit, and abstracted their principle from matter altogether. Thought frees itself wholly from the bondage imposed upon it by the senses, denies the finite world, and affirms its own infinity. It declares that change, beginning and ending, genesis and decay, are unthinkable, therefore impossible. How can that which is not begin to be? How can that which is cease to be? The world in which we live is a delusion of the senses; its changing and manifold forms are a mere appearance, and have no real existence; only being is; there is no becoming (therefore no progress).

Xenophanes, the founder of the school, expressed its principle theologically as the one God, in opposition to the polytheism of his age; Parmenides, a disciple of Xenophanes, and a deeper thinker than his master, developed the doctrine metaphysically; Zeno, a disciple of Parmenides, perfected it dialectically. Thus three generations worked together in the formation and development of this system.

Xenophanes.—Xenophanes was born at Colophon, in Asia Minor, but in what year is uncertain. We know from his writings that he was a contemporary of

Pythagoras, whom he outlived. It is said that his removal to Elea, in Lower Italy, where he died at an advanced age, gave its name to the school.

He wrote in verse, like all the older philosophers; but only a few fragments of his poems remain. In these he enunciates the doctrine that one God rules the world, for Deity is the highest, and the highest can only be One: "One God there is, among gods and men the greatest; neither in body like to mortals, nor in mind. . . . With the whole of him he sees, with the whole of him he thinks, with the whole of him he hears. . . . Without exertion, by energy of mind, he sways the universe. . . . . That he abides forever in the same state, without movement or change from place to place, is evident. . . . But mortals fancy that gods come into being like themselves, and have their senses, voice and body. But of a truth, if oxen and lions had hands, and could draw with their hands, and make what men make, then horses would paint the images of gods like unto horses, and oxen like unto oxen, and shape their bodies also after the similitude of their own limbs."

To comprehend what this meant in that old Greek world, we must reproduce for ourselves its conditions, sensuous and intellectual; must go back, if possible, to its consciousness. To us it seems little to say that God is pure spirit; we have grown up in that belief and conviction. But it was a grand utterance to make in the face of Greek polytheism and anthropomorphism.

Xenophanes censures Homer and Hesiod for presenting the gods like human beings, with the voices and faces, the virtues and vices, of men. Limitation of any kind, physical, intellectual or moral, is unworthy of Deity.

It is possible that Xenophanes meant to affirm the unity of the world at the same time with the unity of God. As he could not harmonize likeness to men with his conception of Deity, so in natural appearances he would seek the ground of their similarity and connection in a force which could not be separated from the world itself. If Deity is One, all things are one, and, in the words of Zeller, "Polytheistic religion becomes philosophic pantheism."

Parmenides.—Xenophanes does not see the difficulty that lies in the acceptance of his point of view; it is Parmenides who recognizes it first. The date of this philosopher's birth is also unknown, but Socrates says in Plato's dialogue of "The Sophist:" "I was present when Parmenides uttered words of exceeding beauty. I was then a young man, and he already advanced in years."

Parmenides is the most important figure in the Eleatic school, and was revered by antiquity for the purity of his character and the depth of his thinking. He exerted great influence in his native city, improving its morals and legislation. He disseminated his philosophic doctrines by means of public lectures and discussions, and embodied them in a poem on Nature, fragments of which are preserved in the works of Plato, Sextus Empiricus, Proclus, and Simplicius. They have been translated into English by Professor Thomas Davidson, and published in the fourth volume of *The Journal of Speculative Philosophy.*

The poem opens with an introduction wherein Parmenides represents himself as borne aloft in a chariot, drawn by coursers that are guided by the daughters of the Sun to the seat of the goddess, who teaches him how to distinguish between the "Truth's unwavering heart that is fraught with conviction," and the "deceptive notions of mortals." Professor Davidson inclines to the belief that Themis, the personification of Justice or Law, is the goddess to whom allusion is made. She discourses first on Truth, which consists in the knowledge that only Being is, that there is no Non-Being, no Becoming.

> "Never it was or shall be ; but the All simultaneously now is
> One continuous one; for of it what birth shalt thou search for?
> How and whence it hath sprung? I shall not permit thee to tell me,
> Neither to think of what is not, for none can say or imagine
> How Not-is becomes Is; or else what need should have stirred it
> After or yet before its beginning to issue from nothing?
> Thus either wholly Being must be or wholly must not be."

From this principle of pure Being, which Parmenides sets up as absolute, he excludes all change, all relation to space and time, all divisibility and movement. It was not, it will not be, it *is* in the eternal present, annulling time.

> "Same in the same and abiding, and self through itself it reposes,
> Steadfast thus it endureth, for mighty Necessity holds it—
> Holds it within the chains of her bounds and round doth secure it."

The "mighty Necessity which holds it" implies a kind of self-limitation on the part of the infinite Being of Parmenides.

> "One and the same are thought, and that whereby there is thinking;
> Never apart from existence, wherein it receiveth expression,
> Shalt thou discover the action of thinking, for naught is or shall be
> Other besides or beyond the existent."

Thinking produces itself in a thought, which is identical with its being, for outside of this great affirmation it is nothing. All thinking is thinking of Being; the *is*, either **ex**pressed or implied, is contained in every affirmation. Being is a thoroughly undivided, homogeneous, perfect whole, which Parmenides compares to a well-rounded sphere, because it holds and comprehends everything, and because thinking is not outside but inside of itself. The senses, therefore, which perceive change and plurality, are deceptive; only thought, which recognizes the necessity of Being, and the impossibility of Non-Being, conducts man to the truth.

To the first part of his poem Parmenides added a second, devoted to the doctrine of Opinion, wherein he seeks to explain the existence of the gods and of the universe from physical grounds. He introduces it with the remark that having finished his discourse "touching the truth," he will now deal with the "notions of mortals." Aristotle says that "being compelled to follow the phenomena, and assuming that the One is according to reason, and plurality according to sense," Parmenides again lays down the two causes as his first principles, hot and cold—meaning, for example, fire and earth. The former of these, the hot, he arranges on the side of Being, the other on that of Non-Being. The light, the fire, is the active principle; the night, the cold, is the passive. The "mixing" of these contraries is effected by the all-controlling Deity, who "gave birth unto Love, foremost of all the gods." Supposing the other principle to be Hate, as Cicero asserts, we have an approach to the doctrine of Empedocles, whose two great physical principles are Friendship and Strife; or, in other words, attraction and repulsion.

Parmenides, seeking to explain the many and the changeable, that which has no existence according to his fundamental principle, only succeeded in developing more completely the contradiction between Being and Appearance, between the eternal and the transitory,—a contradiction that led Zeno, one of his disciples, to attempt the dialectical annihilation of the sensuous world, the world of appearance.

Zeno.—Zeno is said to have been loved by his master like a son. He was the first Greek philosopher who wrote in prose, and was so renowned as a teacher, says Plato, that many came to him for instruction and culture from Athens and other Greek cities. It is reported that he made an unsuccessful attempt to free his country from political tyranny, and was put to death amid tortures which he endured steadfastly.

Aristotle calls him the inventor of dialectic. This dialectic is well described in Plato's dialogue of Parmenides, where Socrates says: "I see, Parmenides, that Zeno is your second self in his writings too; he puts what you say in another way, and half deceives us into believing that he is saying what is new. For you, in your compositions, say that all is one, and of this you adduce excellent proofs; and he, on the other hand, says that the many is naught, and gives many great and convincing evidences of this."

Zeno replies that his writings were meant to protect the arguments of Parmenides, and were addressed to the partisans of the Many, and intended to show that greater or more ridiculous consequences follow from their hypothesis of the Many, if carried out, than from the hypothesis of the existence of the One.

Zeno sought to prove that the many, the changing, all that has relation to space and time, is in itself contradictory, and does not possess true being. His most celebrated arguments are those wherein he denies motion, resting his proofs upon the infinite divisibility of space and of time. He says first that motion is impossible, because a body cannot move or arrive anywhere without passing through an infinite number of intermediate places. Suppose the space to be traversed a mile; this mile can be divided into two parts, and again into two, and so on infinitely. The moving body must pass over these infinite divisions, but the infinite is never-ending; hence it can never reach its goal. It is known that Diogenes the Cynic answered this argument by walking back and forth in silence, regarding this action as a practical refutation of its truth. But Zeno did not deny the sensuous certainty of motion; what he sought was to comprehend it through thought.

His second argument, which I have not space to elaborate, maintains that the pursuer can never overtake the pursued, however swift the one or slow the other. It rests upon the infinite divisibility of time, as the first rests upon the infinite divisibility of space. Aristotle answers both arguments by showing that time and space are not made up of separate points, but are continuous, and that the dimensions of the one must correspond with the divisions of the other; that the infinite in division must be distinguished from the infinite in extent.

Zeno adduced other proofs against the possibility of motion. The contradictions that he developed we meet again in modern philosophy, in the antinomies of Kant.

Melissus of Samos is also mentioned by the ancients as a member of the Eleatic school. Several fragments of his writings are found in Simplicius. His thoughts and arguments resemble those of his master, Parmenides, but are worked out more in detail.

The Eleatic doctrine forms the chief turning point in the history of older speculation. Greek philosophy advanced gradually towards the most abstract of all conceptions, that of pure Being. From this point of view it was impossible to explain plurality or change, or the phenomena of nature. We first see land, according to Hegel, in Heraclitus, who affirms that the truth lies neither in Being nor Non-Being, but in both,—in the Becoming.

"The importance of the Eleatic principle introduced into the fabric of European thought influenced our language through such words as entity, existence, essence. The Eleatics may claim as their own coinage the title of all metaphysics—Ontology, or the Science of Being."—*J. A. Symonds.*

CHAPTER VII.

HERACLITUS.

HERACLITUS, called by later writers "The Obscure," was born at Ephesus, about 500 B. C. He was but slightly esteemed by his fellow-citizens, and esteemed them as slightly in return. The banishment of his friend Hermodorus, whose personal superiority was his chief offence in the eyes of the Ephesians, filled the soul of Heraclitus with scorn and indignation. It was the same principle that led the Athenian democracy to ostracise their greatest men.

Heraclitus wrote a work "Concerning Nature," and deposited it in the temple of Diana at Ephesus. Socrates said that what he understood of it was excellent, and he had no doubt that what he did not understand was equally good, but it required an expert swimmer.

Heraclitus was the first to assert that Being and Non-Being are the same. "Everything is and also is not." "Into the same stream we descend and at the same time we do not descend; we are and also we are not. For into the same stream we cannot possibly descend twice, since it is always scattering and collecting itself again, or rather, it at the same time flows to us and from us." There is nothing firm and enduring in the world, everything is comprehended in continual change. The visible passes into the invisible, the invisible into the visible;

one is replaced by the other as light succeeds darkness. Upper and under, beginning and end, mortal and immortal are the same; everything is one, everything becomes all. From the living come the dead, from the dead the living; from the young the old, from the old the young; the stream never stands still; the clay of existence is continually moulded into new forms.

Heraclitus compares the world to a mixture which must be constantly shaken to prevent decomposition. "Strife is the father of things," he says. Everything exists only in change, and change is a transition from one state to its opposite. From conflict comes existence; from contradiction, union; from discord, harmony; one being produces all, and in the play of conflicting activities maintains all as one. "Unite the whole and the not-whole," says Heraclitus; "the coalescing and the non-coalescing, the harmonious and the discordant, and thus we have the One becoming from the All, and the All from the One."

Heraclitus set up fire also as a first principle. But he must not be ranked with the Ionian physicists. Fire to him is the symbol of the Becoming, the soul as well as the substance of the natural process, existing only in constant change and movement, and thus producing the restless pulse-beat of nature. "The universe always was, and is, and will be an ever-living fire, which is kindled and extinguished according to its own law." Water and earth are but modes of fire; fire passes over them in the "downward way," and they pass over into fire in the "upward way," but the two ways are inseparable.

Man, like everything in the world, comes from fire.

But it is in the soul alone that the divine flame is preserved in its purity. Heraclitus regards the body by itself as an object of horror. The purer the fire, the more perfect the soul; "the dryest soul is the wisest and best." If the fire is polluted, reason is lost, and thus madness is explained; the drunkard is not master of himself because his soul is damp. During this earthly life our souls are dead and buried in us, but at the death of the body they live; and thus, says Heraclitus, life and death are indissolubly united.

Wisdom consists in recognizing reason, which rules everything; "eyes and ears are poor witnesses to men in so far as they have barbarous souls." What our senses perceive is only the fleeting appearance, not essence; the ever-living fire is concealed from us by a hundred veils; that which seems to us dead and mute is in truth the most living and active. The human mind has insight only so far as it participates in divine reason. Most men live like cattle, says Heraclitus; they are born, beget children, and die without finding in life any high aim or significance. He who is wise will recognize that it only depends on himself to be happy; that the world is always as it ought to be, and that he must place himself in harmony with its divine arrangement. He must follow not his own individual opinions, but the common law, the universal reason which rules everything, sacrificing peculiarities and subordinating himself to the idea of the whole.

Heraclitus reaches the grand thought that consciousness of truth is a consciousness of the universal, and that error consists in the separation of thinking from the divine reason in which it participates. He affirms that man must withdraw from the sensuous world, where "everything flows," into the depths of his own spirit, if he would find the steadfast and abiding, the necessity and universality of Being, the essence of thought and of the world. This is what Spinoza terms " contemplating things under the form of eternity."

Zeller says that Heraclitus was the first philosopher to set up common points of view for the total contemplation of nature. To the changeableness and transitoriness of single things he opposed the unchangeable similarity of universal relations, the one divine law, absolute and unconditioned, throughout the universe.

His principle of the Becoming is antithetical to that of Being as held by the Eleatics: but both are alike valid and demand a conciliation. How is this to be effected? Heraclitus does not solve the problem, for he does not explain why everything is comprehended in a continuous flow, except by saying that "everything is fire," which is but another way of expressing the Becoming. Like the Eleatics, he considers the senses unreliable, and appeals from their testimony to that of thought. Like them, he regards the world of nature as a contradiction; but he affirms its reality, which they denied, and finds in this very contradiction the reason of its existence.

To assert, however, is not to prove, and the question returns: Why is all Being Becoming? How are we to harmonize the two principles, and explain the world of nature and its manifold transformations? This is the problem offered to philosophy which Empedocles and the Atomists seek to solve.

CHAPTER VIII.

EMPEDOCLES.

EMPEDOCLES was born at Agrigentum, in Sicily, 490 B. C., and was renowned among the ancients as a philosopher, poet, physician and prophet. Unlike Heraclitus, he took an active part in public affairs, and gained such esteem among his fellow citizens by his efforts towards establishing a free government that they wished to elect him their king, but he refused the honor. The following lines, translated from his writings by Symonds, show the spirit in which he received their proposition: "Friends who dwell in the great city hard by the yellow stream of Acragas, who live in the Acropolis, intent on honorable cares, harbors revered of strangers, ignorant of what is vile, welcome: but I appear before you an immortal god, having overpassed the limits of mortality, and walk with honor among all, as is my due, crowned with long fillets and luxurious garlands. No sooner do I enter their proud, prosperous cities than men and women pay me reverence, who follow me in thousands, asking the way to profit, some desiring oracles, and others, racked by long and cruel torments, hanging on my lips to hear the spells that pacify disease of every kind."

Empedocles refused to be king because he wished to be looked upon as a god. That he possessed great medical skill for that age and wrought some wonderful cures is certain. He is said to have delivered the people of Selinus from a fearful pestilence caused by the fetid exhalations from a marsh, which he drained at his own expense. Upon his appearance afterward at a public banquet he was hailed by the nobles of the city as a god, the friend of Phœbus, the mediator between angry Deity and suffering men. The manner of his death is differently related. According to one legend he suddenly disappeared after a banquet; according to another he jumped into Ætna, but the crater cast up one of his brazen slippers, and this being found, revealed what he meant to hide—the manner of his death.

The fragments of his writings which we possess are mostly from a poem concerning Nature, addressed to Pausanias in these words: "First learn what are the four chief roots of everything that is—fiery Zeus and Heré, and Nestis with her tears, who is the fount of moisture in the world." He thus expressed figuratively the doctrine of the four elements, which he was the first to adopt. In another passage, he calls them "fire, water, earth, and air's innumerable height."

These four primal substances, which he regarded as eternal and unchangeable, constitute the material part of the world. What appears to us as birth and decay is not so really, but only a mixture and separation. How this mixture and separation are produced is the problem. For life no longer resides in matter, as with the old Ionians; and the world of change must be denied, or its phenomena explained by separating a moving force from immovable substance.

Empedocles assumes two moving powers or forces, which he personifies as love and hate, or attraction and repulsion. One tends to life, the other to death; one to unity, the other to discord. They reign alternately at fixed intervals of time, the elements originally forming one including sphere, where love is supreme. But hate gradually asserts its power, and the phenomenal world comes into existence. "When hate or strife has reached the very bottom of the seething mass, and love assumes her station in the centre of the ball, then everything begins to come together and to form one whole—not instantaneously, but different substances come forth according to a steady process of development. Now, when these elements are mingling, countless kinds of things issue from their union. Much, however, remains unmixed, in opposition to the mingling elements, and these malignant Hate still holds within his grasp. For he has not yet withdrawn himself altogether to the extremities of the globe; but part of his limbs still remain within its bounds and part have passed beyond. As Hate, or Strife, however, step by step retreats, mild and innocent Love pursues him with her face divine; things which have been immortal instantly assume mortality; the simple elements become confused by interchange of influence. When these are mingled, then the countless kinds of mortal beings issue forth, furnished with every sort of form—a sight of wonder." Empedocles asserts that human beings were first produced in amorphous masses containing the essence of male and female, but that being afterward divided the two parts yearned for reunion, hence desire and love—a theory worked out by Plato in the Symposium.

Empedocles believed in metempsychosis. He thought that all human souls were fallen spirits, banished to earth for some crime, to be restored to their heavenly birthright by purity of life and expiatory rites. "From what glory, from what immeasurable bliss," he says, "have I now sunk to roam with mortals upon the earth!" The following eloquent passage, translated by Symonds, occurs in the exordium of the poem: "It stands decreed by fate, an ancient ordinance of the immortal gods, established from everlasting, ratified by ample oaths, that when a spirit of that race which has inherited the length of years divine sinfully stains his limbs with blood, he must go forth to wander thrice ten thousand years from heaven, passing from birth to birth through every form of mortal mutability, changing the toilsome paths of life without repose, even as I now roam, exiled from God, an outcast in the world, the bondman of insensate strife. Alas, ill-fated race of mortals, thrice accursed! from what dire struggles and from what groans have ye been born! The air in its anger drives them to the sea, and ocean spues them forth upon the solid land, earth tosses them into the flames of the untiring sun, he flings them back again into the whirlwinds of the air; from one to the other are they cast and all abhor them. * * * * Weak and narrow are the powers implanted in the limbs of men; many the woes that fall on them and blunt the edge of thought; short is the measure of the life in death through which they toil; then are they borne away; like smoke they vanish into air; and what they dream they know, is but the little each hath stumbled on in wandering about the world; yet boast they all that they have learned the whole—vain fools! for what that is no eye hath seen, nor ear hath heard, nor can it be conceived by mind of man."

Like Xenophanes, Empedocles revered Deity as omnipresent and omnipotent, the God of gods, pure mind, holy and infinite, darting with swift thought through the universe from end to end. He does not appear to have made any attempt to reconcile this intuition, or his belief concerning transmigration, with his physical views.

There is a conflict of opinion regarding the value of his philosophy, but it is held in slight esteem by Plato and Aristotle among the ancients, and by Hegel among the moderns. He struck into a way where physics followed him later when he asserted that the primitive elements of things are incapable of qualitative change. He is to be regarded with Leucippus as the founder of a mechanical explanation of nature. But his system has serious faults. He did not explain why there are four elements, or why one force could not at the same time unite and separate substances. Nor could he prevent the two forces that he assumed from encroaching each upon the limits of the other, because, as Schwegler says, "The complete separation of a dividing and unifying power in the movement of the Becoming is an unwarrantable abstraction." The Atomists were more consistent and logical, though their point of view resembled that of Empedocles, and was based upon the same general presuppositions.

CHAPTER IX.

THE ATOMISTS.

LEUCIPPUS and Democritus were the founders of the Atomistic philosophy. Little is known concerning the life of the first; but Democritus, his friend and disciple, was born about 460 B. C. in Abdera. According to the statement of Diogenes Laertius, he was forty years younger than Anaxagoras. He is said to have been very rich, and to have travelled extensively in search of knowledge. He wrote numerous works, of which we possess only fragments. His style was praised by Cicero for its clearness and elevation, and compared to that of Plato. He lived to a great age, ninety or one hundred years.

Aristotle, in the first book of the Metaphysics, describes the general point of view of the Atomists as follows: "Leucippus and his friend Democritus affirm that the full and the void are elements, calling the first Being, and the second Non-Being, and asserting that one is no more than the other." The fullness is composed of atoms, infinite in number and indivisible. Between them is empty space, or the separating intervals which prevent their mutual contact.

Democritus adduced many arguments in support of his doctrine, among others the following: "Motion requires an empty space, for that which is full cannot receive into itself any thing else. Multiplicity and change are thus rendered possible, while at the same time nothing is ascribed to the atoms which the Eleatics denied to being. They are absolutely simple and homogeneous, substance as such destitute of quality. Atoms can only be an object of thought, not of experience; for all which we perceive sensuously is capable of division. Their only difference is quantitative. "They differ in form," says Aristotle, "as A. from N.; in order, as A. N. from N. A.; in position, as Z. from N." They have the like specific gravity, but vary in magnitude, and therefore in weight. All change is change of place, and the sensuous attributes of things are traced back to a quantitative relation between atoms.

These atoms are represented in constant motion; but wherefore is not explained except by saying that the motion is eternal. Since they differ in magnitude and weight, some are forced downward more rapidly than others, and the lighter ones are pushed upward, giving rise to collisions and a rotary motion, which, extending farther and farther, produces an infinite number of worlds. Homogeneous elements come together in this process, not through chance but through necessity, which Democritus set up as a final cause in opposition to the (νοῦς) *nous* of Anaxagoras. "He thus approached as near to the teleology which he scorned," says Zeller, "as it was possible to do from his point of view."

After explaining the origin of the earth, Democritus turned to living beings, and declared that the soul causes their movements; and is therefore composed of the finest and smoothest atoms, or particles of fire distributed through the body. We inhale and exhale soul-atoms, and through this double process life is preserved.

Democritus complained that we know nothing in reality, but at the same time distinguished between obscure and genuine knowledge, the first being gained through the senses, the second through the understanding; one is restricted to changing appearances, the other is an investigation of principles.

In his ethical views he attributed little worth to externals, and argued that happiness can only be found in the right disposition of mind and heart. Man is to enjoy as much and suffer as little as possible. But it does not follow from this that sensuous pleasure is the highest. Only the goods of the soul are worth seeking, those of the body are perishable and unsatisfactory. Democritus recommended content, moderation, purity of thought and deed, as the way to true happiness. Man must limit his desires and his activities to what he is able to accomplish; must be satisfied with what he possesses, and not seek or long after the unattainable. Knowledge gives the highest and purest enjoyment, and that serenity of soul which neither fears death nor earthly calamity.

Schwegler calls the Atomistic philosophy a "mediation between the Eleatic and Heraclitic principles." It asserts with Parmenides the impossibility of the Becoming as a qualitative change, but on the other hand it affirms with Heraclitus the reality of movement, and the relative truth of experience. Through its antithesis of the fulness and the void it expresses the two movements of the Heraclitic Becoming, Being and Not-Being. It embraces in its investigations a wider field of inquiry than any earlier system, and, though one-sided and unsatisfactory, shows nevertheless an advance of thought in its attempt to collect and explain scientifically the empirical facts of nature.

Aristotle praises its logic and the unity of its principles, though he recognizes the impossibility which underlies every Atomistic system of deriving the extended from that which has no extension, indivisible atoms. He also criticises severely the necessity of Democritus, the power behind the atoms, which, though distinguished from chance, is represented as working blindly and without design. Anaxagoras first utters the solving word in his principle of the *nous* (νοῦς).

CHAPTER X.

ANAXAGORAS.

ANAXAGORAS was born about 500 B.C., at Clazomenæ, in Asia Minor. He took no part in public affairs, but devoted himself to scientific pursuits, and soon after the Persian war removed to Athens. There he lived and taught until, accused of impiety, he was compelled to flee to Lampsacus, where he died at the age of seventy-two.

Asia Minor or Italy had been the seat of philosophy hitherto; it was Anaxagoras who first planted it in Athens, where it was to reach the zenith of its glory in the systems of Plato and Aristotle. He was surrounded by a galaxy of great men, many of whom were his personal friends,—Pericles, Thucydides, Phidias, Æschylus, Sophocles, Aristophanes, and Protagoras. Athens was at its height of political prosperity under the administration of Pericles, and the grandeur of its achievements in every field of intellectual activity has never since been equaled.

Hegel speaks of the contrast presented at this time between Athens and Sparta. In Sparta the individual was so wholly merged in the state that he could not attain free development and expression, could not grow morally or intellectually. A principle true in itself was carried out so one-sidedly that its own essence was lost, since the very idea of a state is the voluntary subjection of the individual to the universal will. In Athens, on the other hand, the right of subjectivity was recognized, and every citizen was free to cultivate and develop to the utmost his peculiar talents, and to express himself in whatever way he chose, through statesmanship, or history, or poetry, or sculpture. From this freedom of the individual sprang those immortal works of genius which still challenge our reverential admiration.

Never did any other people in the world express themselves so fully and completely as the Athenians in the age of Pericles. Pericles himself as the head of the State, occupied a unique position,—a quiet, energetic, earnest man, devoting himself supremely to the interests of Athens. Anaxagoras was the friend of Pericles, and was envied, like Aspasia, for enjoying this honor, and exposed to persecution.

Starting from the same point as his predecessors, Anaxagoras reaches the conviction that nature can only be explained through the theory of a divine intelligence disposing and governing everything. Hence, even in the scientific domain, the principle of subjectivity makes itself valid. Aristotle praises Anaxagoras for rising to the conception of a world-ordering reason, and says that in comparison with previous philosophers he appeared like a sober man among the drunken. But to this praise is added censure of the mechanical way in which he applied his doctrine, using the *nous* only when he fell into embarrassment through his ignorance of natural causes.

Plato makes a similar criticism in a well-known passage of the Phædo. Socrates, just before his death, relates how rejoiced he was to hear that Anaxagoras had set up reason as the cause and principle of the world, and how zealously he applied himself to the study of this philosopher's writings, expecting to learn why things are as they are, or, in other words, their final causes. His hopes were disappointed. Anaxagoras used everything else in the way of explanation except the *nous* —fire, air, water, etc. Socrates illustrates the case by saying that Anaxagoras would bring forward his bones and muscles as the reason why he, Socrates, is sitting there in person, instead of the true cause, which is his own will, the opportunity for escape having been offered him by his friend Crito. This opportunity his bones and muscles would gladly have embraced, fleeing to Megara or Boetia, had he not held it better to remain in prison, and submit to the punishment inflicted by the laws. He acknowledges that without possessing bones and muscles he could not do as he thinks best; but to affirm that they are the cause of his action, of his remaining in prison or escaping from it, is to mistake the matter altogether.

Anaxagoras assumes the existence of an infinite number of elementary substances, differing in quality, as particles of flesh, gold, etc. These particles he calls seeds, the name "*homoumeria*" being applied to them later. As there are numberless things in the universe, and not one exactly like the other, so with these "seeds." Their homogeneous union produces what we call the genesis of things; their separation, what we call decay. Change is not qualitative, but mechanical; substance remains the same, but the manner of its composition differs.

Hegel calls the seeds of Anaxagoras "individualized atoms." Originally they existed in a chaotic condition, but after an indefinite period of time the *nous* came, a moving, ordering force, uniting them all into one harmonious whole. This process of formation is explained at length; but it is noticeable that mind is used only in order to move matter, and is conceived more like an impersonal force than a self-conscious intelligence. Nevertheless, Anaxagoras defines it after the analogy of the human spirit, and ascribes to it thinking, which can only be applied strictly to a personal being. Elsewhere he calls it the finest of all things, describing it with the attributes of substance or force. Its activity is represented not as an activity for an end, but as a mechanical movement of matter. This is the point especially criticised.

It could not be expected that Anaxagoras should see the whole bearing of his principle, or how completely it was to revolutionize the old way of thinking. He stands with one foot on the ground of preceding theories, only half-conscious how far he has advanced beyond their basis. He separates the corporeal from the spiritual, but, so far from reconciling the contradiction between the two, he scarcely recognizes its existence. Matter is conceived as the absolutely mixed, and spirit as the separating force; both are united so closely that we cannot question which is first.

But the light, though faint, begins to dawn in the system of Anaxagoras, and is to wax stronger and stronger until with Aristotle it illuminates the whole domain of philosophic research. Anaxagoras closes the old period and opens the new, combining the principles of his predecessors, and setting up his *nous* as an explanation. Its universal character was not at first recognized. It was conceived by the Sophists as the subjective thought of individual man instead of the divine reason in which all participate.

CHAPTER XI.

THE SOPHISTS.

UNTIL the middle of the fifth century B. C., the study of philosophy was limited to the few disciples gathered around its founders in single cities. But at this time a change occurred in the condition of affairs. The brilliant successes attained by the Greeks in their contests with the Persians had awakened as their natural result a passionate striving after freedom, glory, and power. The men who had risked their lives for their country wished to share in the guidance of its affairs, and democracy became the ruling form of government. Athens, through its great deeds, was placed at the ruling centre of Greek national life, and united in itself more and more the intellectual forces and strivings of the age. Within a human generation it attained a degree of prosperity and power, of glory and splendor, unrivaled in history. The traditional means of education no longer sufficed, the claims of the individual increased, special culture was required to lift him above the high intellectual level of his fellow-citizens. Acuteness of intellect was a general characteristic; all were trained through political activity and multifarious intercourse to quick judgment and decisive acting. Through the development of dramatic poetry and artistic oratory, the hearing of all was sharpened for the beauty of language and subtleties of expression. Hence the increased attention paid to eloquence and to rhetoric, and the need that arose for scientific instruction concerning all things useful to civil life.

Hegel, in treating of this period, explains the true meaning of culture. It is a knowledge of the general points of view that pertain to an action or an event, and the ability so to conceive them as to have an immediate consciousness of all their relations. A judge is acquainted with the different legal aspects of a case, the various laws applicable to the particular case under consideration, and sums them up in his consciousness before giving a verdict. In the same way, the cultivated man regards every object from different points of view, and because he sees the matter on all sides conceives it clearly and comprehensively. This culture Greece owed to the Sophists, who taught men not only to argue but to think concerning matters which they accept intellectually.

Philosophy had reached a point where its form must change. Proceeding from observation of external nature it had gradually advanced to the discovery of a spiritual force in the soul itself different from the body which it ordered and ruled. Spirit therefore appeared the higher when contrasted with matter, and man turned his thoughts from the investigation of physical problems to those presented by his own interior nature.

That the right way would be found at first could hardly be expected. Self-exalted by his newly discovered spiritual supremacy, man declared himself the measure of all things, not in the universal but in the individual sense. Every person could determine what was right; truth and goodness ceased to possess absolute validity. Scope was given to unlimited egoism, theoretically and practically. The public and private life of the age mirrors this principle. "Those party struggles which racked Athens during the Peloponnesian war, had blunted and stifled the moral feeling," says Schwegler; "every individual accustomed himself to set his own private interest above that of the State and the common weal, and to seek in his own arbitrariness and advantage the measuring rod of his actions."

The most extravagant ideas were formed concerning popular sovereignty and civil equality. That selfishness which is the curse of all politics seeking aggrandizement bore bitter fruit; moral feeling was blunted, and individuals applying the principle, practiced by the State, towards private instead of public advantage, ceased to regard its welfare as paramount to their own special interests, endangering at once the foundations of law and morality. Frequent changes in the laws seemed to justify the belief that they arose, without inner necessity, from the caprice of rulers. Advancing culture itself tended to weaken the acceptance of old institutions and customs, through keener observation of men and wider knowledge of the world and history.

Scepticism invaded religion; there was much in the old myths opposed to enlightened insight and morality. Man recognized himself as the creator of the gods in their beautiful marble statues, and discovered in his own soul a divinity higher than theirs. Even the development of dramatic poetry tended to shake belief. Beginning at first with Æschylus in a grand contemplation of the moral whole, it descended in Euripides to the analysis of mental conditions and emotional states, subjecting the gods more and more to a human measure. The spirit of revolution and progress which penetrated the age could not be checked and could not fail of expression through philosophy. Hence the peculiar character of Sophistry and the reproaches brought against it by Plato and Aristotle.

Plato complains that it is difficult to define the Sophist correctly. The name was first applied to those paid teachers who pursued wisdom (σοφιστής) as a calling. Plato first and Aristotle afterward narrowed the significance of the term. The Sophist, according to Plato, is a hunter who seeks to capture wealthy young men by promising to teach them virtue; or a trader who traffics in knowledge; or a craftsman who makes gold through controversies, etc., etc. Sophistry is an art of delusion; it consists in knowing how to entangle others in contradictions, in an assumption of wisdom and virtue without possessing either, or even believing in their reality. Aristotle describes it similarly as a science limiting itself to non-essentials, or as the art of making money with mere apparent wisdom.

This judgment passed upon the Sophists by the two greatest thinkers of Greece, colored the opinions of later writers, justifying the assertion of Grote that "few characters in history have been so hardly dealt with as the so-called Sophists." Opinions still differ as to their historical importance. Grote exculpates them from the charge of corrupt and immoral teaching, but asserts that they had "nothing in common except their profession as paid teachers." Hegel, on the other hand, finds that they constitute a distinct school of philosophic thought, and that the character of their work is positive as well as negative.

The previous method of teaching with the Greeks required no teachers except for writing, arithmetic, music and gymnastics. Individual youths who desired wider culture attached themselves to some illustrious man, not for formal instruction, but simply on account of the influence that, without express intention, results from free personal intercourse. The earlier philosophers had no especial school, but imparted their views to a narrow circle composed for the most part of personal friends. With the Sophists we see a new order of things. On one side it is clear that wider knowledge is necessary for those who wish to distinguish themselves in public life; on the other side knowledge is sought, not so much for itself as for practical utility. Sophistry appears to stand on the boundary between philosophy and politics; practice is to be supported by theory, but theory itself becomes little more than a means of help for practice.

The Sophists have been censured for their readiness in adducing reasons and arguments on both sides of a question. But this is not so much a peculiarity of theirs as one belonging to the stage of reflection reached at that time. In the worst action there lies some point of view from which it can be justified and defended. For instance, the duty of self-preservation might be pleaded to extenuate a soldier's desertion on the eve of battle. Excuses might be found even for the crimes of treachery and assassination, and some good motive might be discovered in every evil action.

The Sophist knew that everything can be proved. Gorgias says in Plato's Dialogues: "The art of the Sophists is a greater good than all arts; it is able to persuade as it will the people, the senate, and the judges." The Sophists were acquainted with so many points of view that they could lift into prominence or degrade into insignificance every duty and law hitherto held valid.

The ordinary consciousness is confused, as frequently happens with Socrates, when some opinion or belief firmly held is suddenly brought into collision with others equally valid. Thus, in the instance mentioned of the soldier's desertion, the virtue of bravery which risks life is opposed to the duty of its preservation. Dionysodorus says: "You want Cleinias to be wise. Then you want him to be what he is not, and not to be what he is?—not to be—that is, to perish? Dionysodorus says: "Who lies says what is not, but one cannot say what is not—therefore no one can lie."

These fallacies appear trifling to us now, as Jowett observes, but were not trifling in the age before logic, at a time when language was first beginning to perplex human thought. They show us, farther, how the art of speech assumed more and more prominence until philosophy was almost neglected for rhetoric.

Hegel says that sophistry is a danger that always menaces culture. We moderns admire what Plato would have termed sophistic grounds of action. "Deceive not that you may not lose credit and therefore money."

Similar arguments are brought forward even in sermons and moral discourses to recommend the practice of virtue.

Regarding the accusation brought against the Sophists that they used their talents for money-getting, we easily discover its basis in the prevalent Greek views on this subject. So long as philosophic instruction was confined to friends nothing could be said of pay. Plato and Aristotle regarded it from this point of view. Wisdom, like love, should not be sold, says Socrates, but given as a free gift. Plato and Aristotle maintain that the relation of teacher and scholar is not one of business, but of friendship; the service of the teacher cannot be weighed with money, but can only be returned with love and gratitude. Favored by personal prosperity and sharing the old Greek prejudice against business, they could afford to scorn pecuniary reward for their teaching. But to call the Sophists self-seeking and money-coveting merely because they received pay for the instruction they imparted, is unjust; unjust even from their ideal point of view, since Greek custom permitted painters, musicians, rhetoricians, poets, etc., to win life-subsistence through the work to which they dedicated time and power.

The masses of the people, who, like Plato and Aristotle, regarded the Sophists with disfavor, were farther prejudiced against them as foreigners, "destroyers of the old," innovators and revolutionists. Their gains were doubtless exaggerated; only a few showed themselves mean and avaricious. Protagoras says: "When a man has been my pupil, if he likes, he pays my price, but there is no compulsion, and if he does not like, he has only to go into a temple and take an oath of the value of the instructions, and he pays no more than he declares to be their value."

Zeller thinks that this prejudice against the Sophists as money-makers did more to injure their reputation than anything else. But he also notices a risk which is incurred when instruction concerning the duties of public life is placed exclusively in the hands of teachers who are dependent for support on the pay received; a risk that their activity as teachers may be limited to the wishes and needs of those scholars who are able to seek and pay for instruction. Only a few will see the necessity of studies whose practical application is not immediately apparent. If, from the beginning, Sophistry was inclined to limit instruction to the useful and practical, this one-sidedness must have been strengthened by the dependence of Sophistic teachers on the tastes and wishes of their listeners. We shall therefore find that the Sophists do not teach men concerning the aim of their activity, but seek rather to show the means which secure individual success.

But the question arises: Is there a firm basis to be found anywhere in the doctrines of the Sophists? What is their final criterion of judgment, since to constitute philosophy there must be one? It is the individual self, this particular me, which remains steady when everything else wavers, what Hegel calls "particular subjectivity." To this single self of mine, to *my* pleasure, to *my* vanity, to *my* glory, to *my* honor, I refer everything, intellect, judgment, and all particular conduct. There is no other court of appeal; herein lies the danger of Sophistry. This individual will of mine is erected into an absolute principle; everything else changes, but this remains steadfast. Truth and goodness have only a relative significance; this thing seems true to me and false to another, or good to me and evil to another. The standpoints are as many and as widely different as individuals. Hence the negative attitude of Sophistry towards knowledge and morality.

Zeller calls the Sophists the Encyclopædists of Greece, the *Aufklärer* (clearers-up) of their age, participating in the advantages as well as in the disadvantages of this position. He contrasts their boastfulness and assumption, their unsteady, wandering life, their gold-winning, their mutual jealousies, with the earnest humility of Anaxagoras and Democritus, the unassuming greatness of Socrates, the noble pride of Plato; he finds that their eloquence is but superficial and serves falsehood as well as truth, that their scientific views are shallow, their moral axioms dangerous. But on the other hand he thinks it would be unjust to their real achievements to treat them merely as destroyers. He agrees with Hegel that the principle of subjectivity first makes itself valid in the age of the Sophists. Man reaches the consciousness that it is necessary to act from personal insight and conviction, he loses his veneration for custom and tradition, and will accept nothing as true which he has not himself tested. But he does not at once discover the right direction, the point where he is to place himself in order to preserve his mental and moral equilibrium. He recognizes correctly that tradition as such does not prove the truth of an axiom or the authority of a law; but to conclude therefore that truth does not exist, and that the individual is a law unto himself, is to introduce scientific scepticism and moral confusion.

So, too, in the sphere of religion. The Sophists are not to be reproached that they doubted the existence of the old gods of the Greek world, and saw in them only magnified reflections of the virtues and frailties of human beings. What they needed was to complete denial by affirmation, not to lose faith in religion because they lost faith in polytheism.

Nevertheless, Sophistry, with all its shortcomings, is the fruit and the organ of the most thorough revolution which ever happened in the thought and spiritual life of the Greek nation. This people stood on the threshold of a new era; the view opened into a world, hitherto unknown, of freedom and of culture. Is it strange that they became dizzy on the height so quickly attained, that the feeling of self overstepped all limits, that man, recognizing the origin of laws in the human will, believed himself no longer bound by their authority, that he held everything as subjective appearance because he saw everything in the mirror of his own consciousness?

The one-sidedness of Sophistry could not be avoided. The fermentation of the age drove to the surface many impure and muddy substances, but the human spirit must pass through this fermentation before it could purify itself to Socratic wisdom; and as the Germans without a clearing-up period might not have had Kant, so the Greeks without Sophistry might not have had Socrates and a Socratic school of philosophy.

CHAPTER XII.

INDIVIDUAL SOPHISTS.

PROTAGORAS.—There were many renowned Sophists, but the first and most celebrated is Protagoras of Abdera, born about 490 B. C. Little is known concerning his life, save that it was devoted to study and the pursuit of his calling as a public teacher and lecturer, first in Sicily, afterward in Athens. He was an intimate friend of Pericles, with whom he is said to have had an argument once, lasting the whole day, as to whether the javelin, or the one who threw it. or the one who arranged the game, is guilty of the death of a man accidentally hit and killed. Protagoras, like Anaxagoras, was accused of impiety and banished from Athens. The especial cause of his banishment was a writing beginning with these words: "Concerning the gods, I know not whether they exist or not: for there is much to prevent the attainment of this knowledge in the obscurity of the matter itself, as well as in the shortness of human life." All copies of the work that could be found were publicly burnt in the market-place at Athens, at the command of the state, and so far as we know this is the first recorded instance of such an *auto da fe.* Protagoras was drowned at sea on a voyage to Sicily, either in his seventieth or ninetieth year, authorities differing in regard to his age and the time of his death.

His fundamental proposition as a philosopher is the following: Man is the measure of all things, of that which is that it is, and of that which is not that it is not. Taken in its true sense, this is a grand utterance, but it is at the same time ambiguous. Is it man on the side of his particularity, the accidental individual, who is the measure of all things, or is it the self-conscious reason within him, man on the side of his universality, who is the measure of all things? If the first, then the centre of all striving is the individual with his egotism and selfishness, his petty interests and aims. It was thus understood by the Sophists, and it is the chief ground of reproach brought against their teaching. But Socrates and Plato emphasize the deeper truth contained in the proposition of Protagoras; that man as a thinking, rational being is the measure of all things, that reason, thought, self-consciousness, is not a special characteristic, distinguishing me from my fellow men, but is that in which all participate, the universal substance in which all alike have their spiritual being. The true measure of things is not *my* thought, nor *your* thought, but *thought itself*, the absolute within us, *mine and yours*, whose eternal essence is ever the same, unaffected by our individual will and opinion.

Protagoras, however, according to Plato, saw but one side of the truth contained in his proposition. Starting from the doctrine of Heraclitus, that everything is in a constant flow, he applied it to human thought, and declared that nothing is in itself true or false, but true or false only as it is related to the thinking subject. His illustrations are drawn from the facts of sensuous perception. For instance, it may happen that a wind appears cold to one, warm to another; we cannot, therefore, say of the wind itself that it is either hot or cold. Warmth and cold exist only for us, the feeling, perceiving subject. We have first the assertion that nothing is in itself as it appears; and then, that it is true as it appears, a contradictory affirmation. We can argue with equal justice that the wind is cold, or that the wind is warm ; that is to say, truth is relative, but not absolute.

Protagoras was the first to show how "theses might be defended and attacked, and contradictory propositions maintained on every subject." He made a scientific study of language, distinguishing the gender of nouns, the moods of verbs, etc.

The fallacy of his reasoning and of Sophistic reasoning generally consists in giving objective validity to that which is merely subjective, the sensuous perception, the accidental opinion or caprice of the individual. The wind is not cold in itself because it appears so ; that which is true of it is the appearance only. The whole world of sensuous perception is simply appearance ; we can affirm nothing of it except as it is related to thought, the thinking, self-conscious subject. Here lies the truth of the Sophistic doctrine, a truth developed one-sidedly by Protagoras and his followers, yet fruitful in its effects on the progress of philosophy.

Gorgias.— Another famous Sophist was Gorgias, who came to Athens during the Peloponnesian war as an ambassador from his native city, Leontium, Sicily. He remained there for some time, but passed the latter part of his life in Thessaly, where he died at an advanced age. The approximate dates of his birth and death are respectively, 483 and 375 B. C. He taught the art of rhetoric, describing it as the "worker of conviction." He appears to have been greatly admired and esteemed by his contemporaries, with the exception of Plato, who ridicules his ostentatious appearance, and affirms that rhetoric, as taught by Gorgias, is not an art, but a form of quackery, a mass of poetic figures and brilliant metaphors, intended to corrupt and delude the mind of the listener. It is possible that Plato, in his denunciations, refers less to Gorgias himself than to his followers.

The philosophic doctrine of Gorgias is contained in his work "Concerning Not-Being, or Nature." It was divided into three parts, according to Sextus Empiricus, devoted respectively to the enumeration and proof of the three following propositions: First, that nothing exists; second, that if anything existed it would be unknowable; third, that if it existed and were knowable the communication of the knowledge to others would be impossible. Tiedemann says that Gorgias went much farther than any man of sound common-sense can go. Hegel thereupon replies that one might say the same of any philosopher, for what is called sound common-sense is not philosophy, and is often very unsound, since it is ruled by the manner of thinking, the maxims and prejudices peculiar to the time. Gorgias did go farther than sound commonsense, but so did Copernicus, in the opinion of his age, when he affirmed that the earth revolves around the sun.

The propositions of Gorgias are not so meaningless as they appear. He asserts, first, that nothing exists, because in order to exist, its being must be derived from another or must be eternal. He then goes on to prove that both hypotheses lead to contradictions. If derived from another, it must be either from the existent or the non-existent; but this is impossible according to the Eleatic theory. If eternal, it must be infinite, but the infinite is nowhere, and what is nowhere is not. The proof of his second proposition, that if anything existed it would be unknowable, is as follows: If the knowledge were possible, then all that is thought must exist, and we could not think the non-existent. Scylla and Charybdis, for instance. Gorgias here falls into the idealism of modern times, according to which the world of objective existence is merely the product of subjective thought. He affirms, lastly, that if anything existed, and were knowable, the knowledge of it could not be communicated to others. The eye sees colors, the ear hears sounds, but the notion of color cannot be conveyed by sounds, nor by words, nor can the notion of sound be conveyed by color. How, then, if it is impossible to express through one sense what is conveyed to another, can the same idea be in two persons, as it must be in order to constitute a communication of knowledge, if the persons are different one from the other? The dialectic of Gorgias is based wholly on the contradictory nature of sensuous phenomena, and is unanswerable from the standpoint of any physical theory of the universe.

Other Sophists.—Other well-known Sophists were Hippias and Prodicus. Hippias is described as a man of honorable character and of great learning, distinguished more for rhetorical talent than for his philosophical doctrines. Plato ascribes to him the sentiment that law is the tyrant of men, forcing them frequently to do what is contrary to nature. Prodicus was greatly admired by the ancients. The saying, "As wise as Prodicus," became a proverb. He wrote discourses on moral subjects, but his chief merit rests on the distinctions he made between words of similar meaning, synonyms.

Of the other Sophists we know little, except from the testimony of Plato, who describes them in his dialogues, one as teaching the law of the stronger, that right is might, another as declaring that faith in the gods is the invention of wise and cunning statesmen, their dialectic art deteriorating and their doctrines illustrating more and more the evil consequences resulting from their standpoint, the elevation of the subjective opinion and will of the individual into an absolute standard of thought and action.

CHAPTER XIII.

SOCRATES.

THE age of Socrates was the age of the Sophists; Protagoras and Gorgias were his contemporaries. Socrates is frequently called a Sophist, and is held up to ridicule in the "Clouds" of Aristophanes as the representative of Sophistic doctrines. But his teaching, in reality, is the positive complement of the Sophistic philosophy, whose destructive tendencies he vanquished on their own ground, on the truth implicitly contained in their own principles. "Socrates did not grow out of the earth like a fungus," says Hegel, "but stands in definite continuity with his time, and is not only a figure of supreme importance in the history of philosophy, perhaps the most interesting of all among the ancients, but is a world-historical person. For he represents a turning-point of the human spirit in upon itself in the manner of philosophic thought."

Pre-Socratic philosophy proceeded from observation of nature; the Sophists first deviated from physical inquiries, and made man himself a special object of study. This direction is the ruling one with Socrates; he neglects nature, occupying himself almost exclusively with questions whose solution he refers, not to the accidental will of the individual, but to true knowledge, the absolute essence of spirit. Earlier philosophy was dogmatic, applying itself immediately to the world of nature, and defining its being from single prominent peculiarities. It was therefore one-sided and contradictory, and could not resist the attacks of the Sophists, or satisfy the need of the time.

The basis of the philosophic structure must be laid deeper, contradictions must be compared and reconciled through some common standard, different points of view must be harmonized, thought must grasp the real and permanent beneath the changing appearance. How was this to be accomplished? Socrates answered the problem by developing the content of thought itself through a dialectic process of definition and division, the art of forming concepts. In order to have a clear conception of an object I must be able to grasp together its different peculiarities, not concluding with the Sophists that they are mutually destructive because they contain opposite determinations, but finding that they complete each other through their very contradictions, which are all dissolved in a higher bond of unity. To define the conception of justice or valor, Socrates would start from individual examples, and from these deduce their universal character—their true concepts.

Philosophy, according to this view, begins, not with the observation of external but of internal phenomena; not with physics, but with ethics, the truths revealed by God to human consciousness. The world of nature sinks into the background; self-knowledge is the supreme object of all striving. In the place of dogmatism we have dialectic; in the place of materialism, idealism. The problem of the world is included in the higher problem of self. The question is asked: How can true knowledge be obtained? Socrates offers the first solution, asserting that the standard of human thought and knowledge lies in a knowledge of concepts, which can only be gained by a critical investigation of their essence. Plato concludes that objective concepts, ideas, are in the true sense the only reality; and Aristotle affirms finally that the concept, or form, constitutes the moving power, the soul of things, that the absolutely real is pure spirit thinking itself, that thinking is the highest reality, and therefore the highest happiness for man. "It is thus one principle," says Zeller, "represented at different stages of growth, by Socrates, Plato, and Aristotle." Socrates may be called the swelling germ, Plato the rich blossom, and Aristotle the ripened fruit of Greek philosophy, on the summit of its historical development.

LIFE AND CHARACTER.

The philosophy of Socrates is closely connected with his life and personal character. He was born in the year 469 B. C. His father was a sculptor, and Socrates himself followed this occupation for a time; three draped figures of the Graces, said to be his work, were seen by Pausanias in the Acropolis. His mother was a midwife, and he frequently compares his art to hers, since it consists rather in helping others to the birth of thoughts, than in producing them himself. Little is known of his early education, but he must have participated in all the elements of culture to be found at that time in Athens. In the dialogue of Phædo,

Socrates is represented as passing from the views of the early physicists and of Anaxagoras to his own peculiar point of view; and although Plato's testimony is doubtless influenced by the Platonic doctrine of ideas, it is probable, as Ueberweg says, that Plato transfers from his own thought only that which would naturally follow from the views held by the historical Socrates.

Socrates took part in the military campaigns of Potidæa, Delium, and Amphipolis, during the Peloponnesian war, and was distinguished, not only for his intrepidity and endurance, but for saving the lives of his fellow-citizens, Alcibiades and Xenophon. He never left Athens on any other occasion, except once to attend a public festival. He withdrew from political activity so far as was consistent with his duty as an Athenian citizen, and during the course of a long life held but once a public office. It is noteworthy that in this position he displayed that fearless adherence to what he considered right which characterized all his conduct; he could not be intimidated, either by the wrath of the rulers or of the people, to acquiesce in an illegal measure.

It is uncertain at what time Socrates first began to devote himself to what he regarded as his peculiar mission, the awakening of his fellow-men to moral consciousness and a desire after true knowledge. He is uniformly represented by his followers as a man already advanced in years. His mode of instruction was wholly different from that of the Sophists. Day after day he went to the markets and the public walks, to the gymnasia and the workshops, in order to converse with young and old, with citizens and strangers. He would begin with the topic nearest at hand, the trade of the cobbler, perhaps, or of the blacksmith, then give the discourse such a turn as to elicit from the mind of his listener some truth or thought hitherto undiscovered. This was the great vocation to which he devoted himself unweariedly, contending against the self-conceit, the boastfulness and frivolity of youth, seeking to guide all with whom he came in contact to true self-knowledge and morality.

His own character is described as a model of virtue. "No one," says Xenophon, "has seen or heard anything unworthy of Socrates; he was so pious that he did nothing without the advice of the gods; so just that he never injured any one in the least; so much a master of himself that he never chose the pleasant instead of the good; so discerning that he never failed to distinguish the better from the worse; in a word, he was the best and happiest man possible."

Plato also extols the simplicity, the moderation, the self-control of Socrates, whom he represents as the best man of his time, the most just and full of insight, inspired by the deepest piety, dedicating his whole life to the service of others, and dying a martyr in accordance with what he believed to be the will of God. Other writers dwell upon his Athenian polish and urbanity, his cheerfulness and humor, his real kindness of heart, and describe him as the perfect model of a highly-cultivated man, knowing how to avoid the disagreeable in his intercourse with others and to stimulate into activity whatever was best and most worthy. According to his own testimony, he only became what he was after a long struggle with lower passions and impulses.

"He stands before us," says Hegel, "a finished work of classic art, who has brought himself to this height. In a work of art every feature is designed to bring out one idea, to represent one character, that it may constitute a living and beautiful creation; for the highest beauty consists in the most complete development on all sides of individuality according to one inner principle. The great men of that time are such works of art. The highest plastic individual as a statesman is Pericles, and around him like stars, Sophocles, Thucydides, Socrates, etc., have worked out their own individuality and given it a peculiar character, which is the ruling, innermost principle of their being and culture. Pericles lived only for this aim, to be a statesman; and Plutarch relates that he never smiled or went to a banquet after he devoted himself to statesmanship. Thus did Socrates also, through his art and the power of self-conscious will, develop in himself this definite character, and acquire this skill in his life-vocation. Through his principle he gained an influence still active in religion, science, and right, because since him the genius of inner conviction is the basis which is valid first of all to man."

But Socrates is, nevertheless, a thorough Greek, and cannot be taken as the universal moral standard for all time. Plato in a characteristic scene describes the moderation of Socrates in regard to wine, which was in reality no moderation according to the usual sense of the word, since the simple fact is that he can drink more wine than others without being intoxicated. Was he able to do this, as Hegel intimates, through the power of self-conscious will? His moderation is certainly not asceticism, and his self-control is not self-denial, but consists rather in a state of mental freedom which is never lost amid the seductions of the senses.

Another peculiarity of his character, purely Greek, was his ardent friendship for young men, and his neglect of the domestic relation. Whatever may be the truth in regard to the ill-nature of Xanthippe (and she has not been without her defenders), it is certain that a man like Socrates would have tried the patience of any modern wife or mother. But we must not forget that this was one great blemish of Athenian civilization, — the exclusion of wives, mothers, and sisters from social and intellectual companionship with their husbands, sons and brothers.

On the one side, the peculiarities of Socrates are essentially Greek; on the other, essentially modern. His own personal appearance expressed the contradiction between the outward and the inward, so foreign to the classic ideal. The ugliness of his face and figure, his neglect of beauty of form in his philosophic discourses, and the homely illustrations which he used drawn from the most prosaic trades and occupations, must have offended the artistic instinct of the Greeks, and enhanced for them the singularity of his appearance. Plato represents him, in the Phædrus, as refusing to walk out because he can learn nothing from the trees and from the country.

United with this indifference to the external world was an absorption in his innermost self, which at times seemed half to overpower the clearness of his consciousness. To this may be referred the ecstatic states, described in Plato's Symposium, and that *demonic* revelation, known as the "*Genius*" of Socrates, which he ascribed without farther analysis to divine agency.

Plato and Xenophon mention only *demonic* signs, and nowhere speak as if Socrates believed in a personal demon. Hegel compares the voice heard by Socrates to that prophetic knowledge sometimes evinced by the dying, or those very ill, inexplicable from the standpoint of ordinary consciousness. In the Apology, Socrates says: "Some may wonder why I go about in private, giving advice and busying myself with the concerns of others, but do not venture to come forward in public and advise the State. I will tell you the reason of this. You have often heard me speak of an oracle or sign which comes to me, and is the divinity which Miletus ridicules in the indictment. This sign I have had ever since I was a child. The sign is a voice which comes to me and always forbids me to do something which I am going to do, but never commands me to do anything, and this is what stands in the way of my being a politician."

Had the voice been that of conscience it would have commanded as well as forbidden, and would have been concerned with the moral value and worthlessness of an action, rather than its consequences. One explanation considers it as a kind of practical insight, or tact, an immediate conviction of the suitableness or unsuitableness of certain actions, resulting partly from life-experience, partly from self-knowledge, but transformed according to the spirit of the time into a divine revelation.

Hegel thinks that it occupied the middle ground between the external Greek oracle and the purely internal oracle of spirit, marking the transition of human consciousness from reliance on outward to reliance on inward authority. The Greeks, with all their freedom, did not decide from subjective conviction, but in doubtful matters concerning the state, or mere private affairs, consulted the oracle. They had not reached the modern standpoint which demands the testimony of the spirit within for every decision. It is the principle of Socrates which effects this world-conversion, and Socrates therefore unites in himself the characteristics of Greek and of modern consciousness; "distinguished from all his contemporaries," says Zeller, "by that power of inward concentration, so foreign to his race, through which an invisible breach first took place in the plastic unity of Greek life."

CHAPTER XIV.

THE FATE OF SOCRATES.

IN his seventieth year, Socrates was brought to trial by his fellow-citizens in Athens. The accusation against him consisted of two points: that he was neglecting the gods of the state, and introducing new deities, and that he was corrupting the youth. The accusers were Meletus, a poet, Anytus, a demagogue, and Lycon, an orator,—men of comparative insignificance in the state.

It was contrary to the nature of Socrates to defend himself by means of the artful oratory then practiced in Athens. He relied on the simple truth, and left the issue in the hands of God. His language was not that of a criminal, but of an impartial reasoner who would fain dispel erroneous notions. He would not condescend to address the judges in terms of entreaty. His proud and dignified bearing offended the members of a popular tribunal accustomed to deference and homage from the most eminent statesmen and generals. He was pronounced guilty by a small majority. But according to the Athenian laws he was left free to express an opinion as to the punishment he should receive, this expression being an implied acknowledgment of guilt. He refused to name any punishment, but declared himself worthy of reward as a benefactor of the state. Finally, however, he yielded to the entreaties of his friends, and consented to a fine of thirty minæ, which he could pay without owning himself guilty. He was thereupon condemned to death.

The execution of the sentence was delayed thirty days, until the return of the sacred ship from Delos. Socrates employed the time in social intercourse with his friends, retaining through the whole period his accustomed cheerfulness and serenity. He scorned, as unworthy, the means of escape offered by his friend Crito, believing that, as a citizen of the state, he ought to obey its laws and submit to its sentence of death. This seems slightly at variance with his refusal to acknowledge himself guilty. But the refusal was based on a higher law than that of the state, "The unwritten laws of God that know no change." Conscious of the right, Socrates would not yield. He acknowledged the sovereignty of the people with this one exception.

The competence of the court is presupposed to-day, and the sentence is executed without farther formalities; regard is paid rather to the act than to the disposition of the subject. But the Athenians required that the decree of the court should be sanctioned by the convicted man himself, who was left free to estimate his own punishment and thereby acknowledge the justice of his sentence. Socrates, who stood acquitted before the bar of his own individual conscience, opposed this acquittal to the conviction of the judges.

But the first principle of a state is this: that there is no higher reason, or conscience, or justice, than that which the state recognizes. Hence the fate of

Socrates is truly tragic, like the fate of Antigone. There is a conflict between his duty to the state and his duty to himself; between the law of the land and the diviner law within his own breast. Two moral forces come into collision one with the other, and this is what is meant by the tragic and tragedy. The fate of Socrates is not merely personal; it is the tragedy of Athens, of Greece. Two rights, equally valid, are opposed to each other; the right of objective freedom secured by life in and for the state, and the right of subjective freedom, of the individual conscience. The Athenian people had reached that point in their development when the state, the outward manifestation of their national spirit, no longer satisfied the inner needs of the individual. In condemning Socrates to death they committed the injustice of making him pay the penalty of that which was historically the fault of all, if fault it were.

Plato has given us a touching and beautiful picture of the last hours of Socrates. They were passed in quiet converse with his friends on the subject of immortality. When the final moment came he calmly drank the cup of poisoned hemlock, conscious that death would strengthen his influence and give to his life and work the highest stamp of truth.

Different opinions have been held by different writers as to the causes and the justice of his condemnation. Hegel believes that both Socrates and the Athenian people were alike innocent and alike guilty; that Socrates was the representative of the modern spirit, the principle of subjectivity, the individual conscience, as opposed to the unreflecting Greek morality resting on the basis of tradition.

But the Athenian people themselves had advanced beyond their old standpoint; they too, as well as Socrates, were in part children of the new time. The moral life of Greece rested originally on authority; Socrates substituted instead personal conviction. The individual is not simply to obey the law, he is to discover, in and for himself, its reason and its justice. Socrates spent his life in examining the current notions respecting morals, seeking their causes and testing their truth. The examination led him to the same results, essentially, as those which were established by custom and tradition. Nevertheless, his attitude towards the old Greek morality was a critical attitude. If man is to follow his private convictions he will agree with the popular will only when it agrees with his own. If the two conflict there is little doubt what side he will espouse. This is the principle avowed by Socrates in the celebrated declaration that he would obey God rather than the Athenians.

Plato says there was a general belief that the teaching of Socrates was of a dangerous character, and he adds that it was then impossible for any one to speak the truth in political matters without being persecuted as a vain babbler, a corrupter of youth. It is certain, from the testimony of Xenophon and Aristophanes, that the prejudice against Socrates was not confined to the masses, but was shared by men of influence in the state. Aristophanes, an enthusiastic admirer of the "good old times," was bitterly hostile to the new ideas introduced into Athens by the Sophists, among whom he classed Socrates as the most dangerous.

Aristophanes and the Aristophanic comedy are as much a product of the time as Socrates and the Socratic philosophy: both are stars of lesser and greater magnitude in that brilliant galaxy which constitutes the glory of Athens. Aristophanes, though sincere in his advocacy of the old and his scorn for the new, was himself infected by the very spirit which he attacks, the spirit of progress. His representation of Socrates in the "*Clouds*" though an unmistakable likeness, is not only exaggerated, but essentially false, "and can only be designated," says Schwegler, "as a culpable misunderstanding, and as an act of gross injustice, brought about by blinded passion; and Hegel, when he attempts to defend the conduct of Aristophanes, forgets that while the comic writer may caricature, he must do it without having recourse to public calumniation."

The charge brought by Aristophanes against Socrates was three-fold: that he devoted himself intellectually to useless subtleties; that he rejected the Athenian gods; and finally, that he was able by Sophistic reasoning to gain for the wrong side the victory over the right, to make the weaker argument appear the stronger. That the comedy of Aristophanes was the originating cause of the persecution directed against Socrates is improbable, yet it doubtless expressed what others thought, and could not have been without its influence, for twenty-four years later, when Socrates was legally accused and convicted, it was upon similar grounds to those brought against him in the "*Clouds.*"

All the charges seem to rest upon misunderstandings and false inferences. For instance, it was said that he rejected the gods of the State, and substituted in their place a deity of his own, his demon. This was untrue. He worshipped in the Athenian temples like his fellow-citizens; his demon was not a new god, but a private subjective oracle. Socrates, according to Hegel, is the hero who substitutes for the Delphic god and the Delphic oracle this principle: man must find in himself that which is true. The thinking self-consciousness, not the external oracle, is the final authority. This inner certainty was in truth a new faith differing from the old, but not a new god in the sense meant by his accusers.

It was also said that Socrates had corrupted the Athenian youth. Here again he is identified with the Sophists; the charge is the same as that brought against their teaching. The views of Critias and Alcibiades are unjustly ascribed to his influence; and it is concluded that he taught men to despise their parents and relations because he counselled Anytus to educate his son for something higher than the leather business. The inference is unfair, though it is a delicate matter for a third person to interfere in the relation between parent and child.

Nothing in the shape of actual deeds could be laid to the charge of Socrates. He conscientiously fulfilled his duties as a citizen, and never transgressed the laws of the State. His political theories did not correspond with the existing Athenian institutions, but this was not a crime. He did not believe in awarding power by lot or election, but according to the qualifications of individuals. This may have led to his being suspected of aristocratic leanings by the Athenian democracy. But it could not affect the purity of his character as a citizen. Nevertheless, the whole character of his philosophy, the demand for self-knowledge, the inward turn given to thought, must have weakened in himself, and in his disciples, that attachment to political life which was the soul of Greek activity. Even his demon, his subjective oracle, was dangerous in a country where oracles had not only a religious but a political significance.

Zeller calls Socrates the precursor and founder of our moral view of the world; but adds, that to one starting from the old Greek view of the state and of right, his condemnation cannot appear altogether unjust. The truth was that in Athens itself the old morality was decaying, and that Socrates simply entered into the spirit of his time, trying to reform it by means of itself, instead of uselessly attempting to bring back a type of culture that was gone forever. It was a mistake to hold him responsible for the corruption in faith and morals which he was trying to check in the only way possible. Zeller thinks that his condemnation was not only a great injustice according to our conception of right, but was a political anachronism according to the standard of his own time. A reformer who is truly conservative is attacked by nominal and imaginary restorers of the good old times. The Athenians, in punishing him, gave themselves up for lost; for in reality it is not for destroying, but for attempting to restore morals that he is punished.

Aristophanes and his followers took one way to rebut the Sophists; Socrates took another. He too, like the Sophists, emphasizes the principle of subjectivity: but he shows that the truth lies not in the feeling of self, which is egotistic and exclusive, but in the idea of self, which is universal and comprehensive. Confounded with the Sophists by his accusers, the higher principle of Socrates was misunderstood and misinterpreted. The spirit of Athens was divided within itself; its internal rupture was reflected in its declining strength and power, and finally it yielded its independence, and became subject, first to Sparta, then to Macedonia.

Socrates died twenty-nine years after the death of Pericles, and forty-four years before the birth of Alexander. He witnessed the glory and the decline of Athens, its culminating point of splendor and the beginning of its ruin.

CHAPTER XV.

THE SOURCES AND CHARACTERISTICS OF THE SOCRATIC PHILOSOPHY.

SOCRATES committed nothing to writing, and our knowledge of his doctrines is derived from the accounts of Xenophon, Plato and Aristotle. Though it is doubtless true that in Plato's Dialogues the thoughts of Plato himself are frequently placed in the mouth of Socrates, the elements peculiar to each are easily discernible. Plato's picture of Socrates agrees substantially with that of Xenophon in those dialogues wherein he claims to be true to facts, the Apology and the Symposium. Socrates had been dead six years when Xenophon wrote the Memorabilia and the Symposium, partly from his own recollection, partly from that of his friends. He was present in person at some of the scenes which he describes; when he was not present he mentions his authority. But Xenophon appears to have been a practical man, deficient in the philosophical sense; his representation of Socrates is therefore one-sided. He emphasizes the ethical, but neglects the scientific side of the Socratic teaching. It was the union of the two that constituted its peculiarity.

Socrates recognized that morality must be established on a scientific basis before reform is possible. I must not only do what is right; I must do it with a clear consciousness that it is right. Socrates could not distinguish between morality and knowledge; in this, as Zeller observes, he was the child of his age. He sought to reform morals by means of knowledge; and the two were so closely associated in his own mind that he could find no object for knowledge except human conduct, and no guarantee for conduct except knowledge. Hence the deep importance attached to the personality of the thinker, the impossibility of considering the philosophy of Socrates apart from his life and character.

"In Socrates commences an unbounded reference to the person," says Hegel, "to the freedom of the inner life." This is the source of his one-sidedness; he directs all his activity and striving towards morals, and neglects the other sciences. He teaches each one to find as the essence of his own individual being the absolute and universal concept of the good. Consciousness turns inward upon itself, and tests the validity of every moral axiom by an inner standard of right. That it is a decree of the state or the will of the gods is not enough; the moral consciousness asks: Is it true in itself? This return into itself is the highest bloom of the Athenian spirit, a point of culture not reached by the Spartans. But it is fraught with danger. It is the isolating of the individual from the universal, the care of man for his single self at the cost of the state, a higher and more comprehensive self. Morality wavers when man makes for himself, individually, his own laws and maxims.

But Socrates penetrated to the kernel of the matter, and found at the basis of self-consciousness an absolute moral authority. He taught men to find the good and the true within their own thought. That knowledge is elicited from the mind itself, that it comes from within and not from without, is a thought contained in the doctrine of Socrates, but developed more fully by Plato. No external power can force a man to think, he must think for and from himself. To learn is only to become acquainted with external things through experience. But the knowledge of universals, the only true knowledge, belongs to thought. Nothing is valid, according to Socrates, without the inner testimony of the spirit. Hegel thus expresses it: "As it is said in the Bible, flesh of my flesh and bone of my bone, so that which is true and right to me must be spirit of my spirit." There is that within me, planted by nature, belonging to me as a particular individual, the selfish self; there is that within me, higher and holier, a part of the divine reason, belonging to me as an immortal person, the unselfish self. Socrates opposed the second to the first, man the universal to man the particular. The Sophists insisted upon the feeling of self, which is egotistic and exclusive; Socrates insisted upon the idea of self, which is universal and inclusive, "the true equalizer of the human race."

His philosophy starts from the Delphic oracle, "Know thyself," and involves a thorough sifting and testing of the general concepts found within the mind. The majority of men confine themselves to suppositions and traditionary facts, whose accuracy they neither question nor examine. They think themselves wise when in reality they know nothing. This is the meaning of the Delphic oracle that calls Socrates the wisest of men, wisest in this, that he is conscious of his own ignorance. To possess this consciousness is most helpful to the seeker after truth, who must have an open eye, a single purpose, and an honest mind to receive it when it comes.

Socrates taught men to think for themselves, to analyze their language and thoughts, to test their opinions, to reason from the particular and contingent to the universal and necessary. Instead of vague notions, he sought to obtain correct concepts of every object, by considering it on all sides, under different points of view, that his knowledge of it might be true instead of imaginary. The soul of his teaching is contained in the principle that true knowledge must proceed from correct concepts. The ordinary way is to accept things as they appear to the senses; but when man begins to reflect he begins also to correct his sensuous impressions by means of thought. What is thought? Can you think a single thing, a maple, for instance, without including in your thought the class, or genus tree, to which it belongs? Does not the essence of thinking consist in having something more present to the mind than that which ostensibly claims the attention? This something more is what Socrates seeks to analyze and define, the general concept as distinguished from the particular sensuous impression.

According to Aristotle, in his Metaphysics, Socrates introduced the method of inductive reasoning and of logical definition, which constitutes the basis of scientific investigation. How these elements stand related to his fundamental principle of self-knowledge will be shown presently.

His method was not something clearly defined in his own consciousness, but a natural manner of philosophizing and imparting instruction peculiar to himself. He sought first to convince men of their ignorance. Nothing is more fatal than to believe you know what you do not know. Nothing is more essential than to distinguish between what you know and what you only think you know. Self-examination is a preliminary step to the attainment of true knowledge; self-delusion is a frequent source of error. Socrates by a series of skillful questions exposed the last, and stimulated men to attempt the first. Apparently ignorant and eager to be instructed by those with whom he converses, he accepts their opinions only to entangle them afterwards in contradictions and absurdities, deducing unexpected consequences, and confusing them more and more until finally their supposed knowledge vanishes. This is the celebrated Socratic irony, the critical factor in the Socratic method, assuming its peculiar form from the presupposed ignorance of the one who uses it as an instrument. The subject upon whom it is practised discovers that he knows nothing, and regards all his previous notions and beliefs distrustfully. It is not a sceptical denial of knowledge on the part of Socrates, but an acknowledgment of his own ignorance, and a discovery of the ignorance of those to whom he applies his testing process. "The idea of knowing was an infinite problem to Socrates," says Zeller, "opposite which he could only be conscious of his own uncertainty."

Socrates, like the Sophists, questions all that had previously passed for truth; but he goes farther, he strikes out a new road for its attainment, leading to a new world of thought, whose conquest is reserved for Plato and Aristotle, but whose discovery is due to Socrates himself. Not finding in himself what he sought, he applied to others; love of knowledge is an impulse to friendship, and the blending of the two constitutes the Socratic Eros. By a kind of art that he calls intellectual midwifery, he sought to help into the world thoughts that lie latent in every one's consciousness. This is the positive side of his interrogatory analysis, an attempt to produce real knowledge, which according to his idea and method can only proceed from true concepts.

His method is that of induction. Starting from the simplest object and the most common notions concerning it, he analyzes them so thoroughly as to bring out the opposition which each contains within itself, or in relation to some other; corrects one-sided assumptions by additional observations; and succeeds finally in separating that which belongs to the essence of the object from that which is accidental and contingent. It is a process of definition, the art of forming concepts. It is also a culture of self-consciousness, the development of reason. The child and the savage dwell in a world of concrete single representations; the adult and the civilized man live amid thoughts and abstractions. Illustrations that appear tedious and trivial to us in our present stage of reflection were essential to clearness of expression in the age of Socrates.

The important element in his dialogues is their method, the fact that what were formerly unexplained hypotheses and unconscious guess-work is now arrived at by a process of thinking. His investigations are directed mainly towards the necessity of knowledge and the nature of morality, towards moral and intellectual self-analysis. The critical discussions in which he engages oblige the speakers to consider what their notions imply, and the aim of their actions.

The problem of philosophy for Socrates, according to Aristotle, is to seek for the essence of virtue, and virtue is regarded as a knowing. Socrates seeks to define the concept of temperance, of valor, of justice, because according to his idea a knowledge of their real essence constitutes the only safe moral guide. Schwegler characterizes the Socratic method "as the skill by which a certain number of given, homogeneous and individual phenomena was taken, and their logical unity, the universal principle which lay at their basis, inductively found. This method presupposes the recognition that the essence of the objects must be comprehended in the thought, that the conception is the true being of the thing. Hence we see that the Platonic doctrine of ideas is only the objectifying of this method which in Socrates appears no farther than a subjective dexterity. The Platonic ideas are the universal concepts of Socrates posited as real individual beings."

CHAPTER XVI.

THE SOCRATIC ETHICS.

THE leading thought of the ethics of Socrates is expressed in the sentence: All virtue is true knowledge. "Socrates, by laying down thought, or more strictly self-consciousness, as the groundwork of ethics," says Prof. Ferrier, "supplies the truest of all foundations for a system of absolute morality, and contains the germ of all the ethical speculations, whether polemical or positive, which have been unfolded since his time."

We cannot do right without knowing what right is; to know it and not to do it appeared impossible to Socrates. No man, according to his theory, is voluntarily vicious. If he knew that thinking was his real self, his real nature, and that appetites and passions are enslaving forces, he would aim at their restraint, and at the preservation of his true being and personality. Man does not pursue evil unless he thinks it good for himself, unless he mistakes the essence of his own nature, and believes that it consists of sensation instead of thought. Right action follows necessarily from a knowledge of the right, according to the Socratic principle; wrong action, from an absence of knowledge. As regards the virtue of bravery, Socrates argued that he who recognizes the true nature of an apparent danger and the means to meet it, has more courage than he who does not. Nothing is more essential morally than self-knowledge ; because he who knows himself truly will unfailingly do what is right, while he who is ignorant of himself, or who mistakes apparent for real knowledge, will do wrong. With Socrates, knowledge is not merely an indispensable condition, and means of help to virtue, but it is the whole of virtue.

Plato and Aristotle correct this one-sidedness. Aristotle objects that Socrates does not distinguish between the intellectual and the emotional parts of the soul, that he deprives our virtuous affections of the warmth and spontaneity by which they are characterized. What is wanting in Socrates is the side of subjective reality which we call the heart. Knowledge is essential to virtue, but is not the whole of virtue, or virtue would belong only to thought, to the intellect alone.

The experiences of the time convinced Socrates that tradition and custom, even the authority of the laws, could not oppose moral scepticism ; that the basis must be laid deeper, that the activity of man must be guided by clear and definite knowledge. If the question is asked, Knowledge of what ? Socrates replies, Of the Good. But what is the good ? The good, according to his definition, is the concept of knowledge treated as an aim, or knowledge itself in its practical application ; an explanation indeterminate enough to admit of various interpretations. Socrates at one time explains the good as the useful, and apparently recommends virtue because it is most richly rewarded by God and man. At another time he qualifies this statement by saying that virtue is useful because it is connected with the health of the soul, the divine part in man, the seat of reason.

It is certainly a contradiction, as Zeller says, to explain virtue as the highest aim of life, and at the same time to recommend it on account of the advantages it brings. But this contradiction proceeds from the abstract character of the concept of virtue, and the impossibility of deriving definite moral activity from the general principle that virtue is a knowing. Kant is not wholly free from the same inconsistency. He rejects most decidedly every moral standard based on experience, and yet, in determining the maxims suited to the principle of universal legislation, determines them according to the consequences which would follow were they universally adopted. The defect in the ethics of Socrates is not so much a want of moral value as of scientific reflection.

Though accident in a great measure guided the discourses of Socrates, there were three points, according to Xenophon, that he treated with especial preference. The first was the independence of the individual through the limitation of his wants and desires; the second was the ennobling of the life of the soul through friendship; the third and most important was the furtherance of the common weal by an ordered life in and for the state. Man, according to Socrates, only becomes master of himself through freedom from needs, and the exercise of his thinking faculty; if dependent on bodily conditions and enjoyments, he is a slave.

Socrates did not shun sensuous pleasures, but was

able to preserve in the midst of them perfect control of himself and of his thought. A thorough Greek, he aimed at moderation and freedom of mind rather than asceticism. He appreciated highly the worth of true friendship, affirming that it was conformable to man's nature, and necessary for mutual help and interchange of ideas. So far as it proceeds from human needs and wants it is based on utility; but Socrates conceives it also in its ideal form, existing only for the sake of the good. In his low estimation of marriage and the office of woman in the household, he agreed with his fellow-countrymen, and speaks " like the husband of Xanthippe rather than the friend of Aspasia." Yet he expressly acknowledges his indebtedness to one woman, Diotima, and says that she was his teacher in the love of wisdom, or philosophy. His own conduct shows little regard for domestic life. He considers the state and not the family, as the chief object of moral activity, and here again he is purely Greek. He not only requires the most unconditional obedience to the laws, but wishes everyone of ability to take part in their administration, since the welfare of individuals depends on the welfare of the community.

This is in accordance with the old Greek view of the state; but he departs from it widely in other respects. He demands that everyone who aspires to be a statesman shall prepare himself by a thorough course of self-analysis and discipline, and only recognizes a right and a capacity to discharge political duties when these conditions have been fulfilled. He believes that where the rule of the majority prevails an upright man can do nothing but return to private life. In place of equality, or an aristocracy of birth and wealth, he would substitute an aristocracy of intelligence, like Plato in the Republic.

These ideas brought him into collision with the Athenian democracy. While insisting on obedience to the laws, he at the same time tests their validity by an inner standard set up by himself, the individual conscience. This contradiction is not peculiar to Socrates, but is manifested at once if one seeks to make a law of the state, or any rule of conduct absolute. Even the command, "Thou shalt not kill," is conditioned by circumstances. The same consciousness that recognizes this as an imperative duty, impels one to battle bravely in defense of his country, or to slay his country's enemies. The laws of the land must be obeyed, but there are times and occasions when disobedience is sublime, and lifts the individual to a height of moral grandeur ordinarily unattainable. This was the case with Socrates himself, and the Antigone of Sophocles. But the individual must not set up his arbitrary will against the will of the state, unless he possesses an insight into the eternal principles of law and justice and morality, and decides according to their dictates instead of following his own subjective liking and inclination.

This relation between the subjective will of the individual and his objective will as embodied in the state, is more a matter of conscious reflection to-day, than it was in the time of Socrates. It was misunderstood by some of his favorite disciples, notably Alcibiades and Critias, one of whom became the enemy and betrayer of his country, the other its opponent and tyrant. They lived in accordance with a one-sided interpretation of the Socratic principle of subjectivity, and cast upon their teacher and his doctrines a discreditable reflection wholly undeserved. For the aim of Socrates, in the self-culture of the individual, was not that of the Sophists, to advance private interest and acquire personal power and dexterity; but to attain true knowledge, and thereby establish the sovereignty of virtue and the well-being of the community. What he sought was to reform the state rather than the means by which it might be governed.

It is uncertain whether Socrates went beyond the common Greek view of morality, inculcating good towards friends, but permitting evil towards enemies. In one of the earliest dialogues of Plato, he is made to say that wrong-doing cannot be permitted even towards one from whom wrong-doing has been suffered. Whether this sentiment is Plato's own or that of historical Socrates, is undetermined.

As to the disgrace that was generally attached to trade and commercial pursuits by the Greeks, Socrates held that any useful activity was honorable, and that idleness alone ought to call forth shame.

Nature.—In his view of nature he refers all physical phenomena to man as their highest end. "He dwells on the Creator rather than the creation," and shows what care has been taken to provide for human needs and wants. He argues that a belief in God and providence would not be inborn in men of all conditions and times if it were not true. The founder of a scientific doctrine of ethics, he is the founder also of that ideal view of nature, which in spite of all abuses and objections has proved itself of value in the study of empirical phenomena.

The adaptation of means to ends in the world of nature, its reasonable arrangement, led him to the conception of the one Supreme Being who sustains to it the relation of soul to body. Yet he frequently speaks of the gods as many, in accordance with the popular faith. He discussed the question of existence after death, and considered it highly probable. "Happiness, virtue, knowledge,—this was the Socratic trinity," says Dr. Lord, "the three indissolubly connected together, and forming the life of the soul,—the only precious thing a man has, since it is immortal."

CHAPTER XVII

THE PARTIAL DISCIPLES OF SOCRATES.

A SPIRIT like that of Socrates could not fail to produce a lasting impression on his immediate contemporaries and followers, an impression, too, of the most varied character, due in part to the lack of system in his philosophy, in part to the convictions and beliefs peculiar to individuals. Many simply perceived and were influenced by his logical personality, his pure character and lofty moral maxims. Xenophon, whose honest integrity and genuine worth win our admiration, depicts Socrates in the most glowing colors as a man and a moralist, but leaves untouched the profounder phases of his thought. A few looked deeper; but even they conceived the Socratic theories one-sidedly, fastening on those which they understood best, and adding others from older systems of philosophy. One thinker alone, Plato, comprehended his master fully, and developed to rich fruition the truths explicit and implicit in the doctrines of Socrates.

Four Socratists besides Plato founded schools of philosophy: Euclid, Phaedo, Antisthenes and Aristippus. Euclid and Phaedo are closely related, and confine themselves chiefly to questions concerning the dialectic of Socrates; Antisthenes and Aristippus, on the other hand, neglect everything but the ethical side of his teaching, understanding and expounding it in different senses, diverging widely not only from Socrates, but from each other.

Socrates defined the object of man's striving as a knowledge of the Good, but he left it for each to determine in what the Good consists and how it is to be pursued. Different theories and different modes of interpretation naturally followed from a principle so abstract. The mission of Socrates was simply to bring men to true wisdom, and to prove that it begins with knowledge of self, including but not included by the knowledge of the world. From this time henceforth philosophy no longer asks, What is nature?—but, What is truth? Man becomes conscious not only of a contradiction between himself and the outer world, but of a contradiction in his own interior being, in thought itself. This was the service of Socrates, and it was impossible for one man to do more than to thus prepare the ground for the munificent harvest afterward reaped by Plato and Aristotle.

THE MEGARIAN SCHOOL.

The Megarian school is named from its founder, Euclid of Megara. He must not be confounded with the Alexandrian mathematician who lived a century later. It is related that when the Athenians and Megarians were at war with each other, he used to steal into Athens at night disguised as a woman, risking his life to hear and converse with Socrates. He was noted both for his obstinacy and calmness in disputing. Once when an adversary cried out in wrath:

"I will die if I do not avenge myself upon you"; Euclid replied, "I will die if I do not so soften your anger by the mildness of my speech that you will love me instead." Euclid was present at the death of Socrates, but after that event returned to Megara, accompanied by many of the Socratists, who remained abroad until the tide of opinion turned at Athens, and the accusers of Socrates were themselves punished.

In his philosophy, Euclid combined the Eleatic principle of being with the Socratic ethics, and affirmed that the Good is one, though disguised under many names, as intelligence, God, thought, etc. The Good alone is; what is opposed to it is not, has no real being. The senses are false witnesses; they show us multiplicity, delusive and changing appearances. Thought alone is able to grasp the immutable essence of things.

The Megarian school was kept up for a time after the death of Euclid, but exercised little influence on the course of philosophy. Eubulides, one of its best known leaders, and a disciple of Euclid, was noted for his sophisms. The Greeks were fond of finding the contradictions that underlie our ordinary speech and representations. Each sentence is a unit, but at the same time consists of a subject and predicate differing from each other; being and non-being are contained in language and in thought. But the common consciousness is confused by an arbitrary separation between the positive and negative elements of a sentence, not perceiving that truth is only to be found in the unity of opposites. "If any one confesses that he lies, does he lie, or tell the truth?" Here is a dilemma like that of Sancho Panza, who in his character of ruler and judge had to decide the following case: A rich man had erected a bridge for the benefit of travelers, and near by a gallows, granting a free passage to any one on condition that he would say truly whither he was going and agree to be hanged if he spoke falsely. One came finally, who in response to the question whither he was going answered, to be hanged on the gallows near the bridge. The owner was in great perplexity. If the man were hung he would have spoken the truth; if he were not hung, he would have spoken falsely. Sancho directed that the milder interpretation be placed on the case, and that the man should be permitted to cross the bridge. The Megarians delighted in similar puzzles, but did not solve them as satisfactorily as Sancho. Carried to a higher point of acuteness and subtlety by the Sceptics, they finally led to absolute negation of all knowledge and reality.

Stilpo was a member of the Megarian school, but united with its doctrines other tendencies belonging to the Cynics. Diogenes Laertius says that he so far surpassed all others in acuteness of speech that the whole of Greece contemplating him was in danger of becoming Megarians. His character was held in the highest veneration. When Megara was taken and plundered he was questioned as to his loss, and replied that he had seen no one carrying away science. A condition of apathy was his highest moral ideal. He thought that the wise man should be sufficient to himself, not even needing friends in order to be happy. When made acquainted with the vicious life led by his daughter, he replied that if he could not bring her to honor neither could she bring him to dishonor.

Phaedo, a favorite disciple of Socrates, founded a school in Elis, resembling the Megarian in its character and tendency. He is the person represented by Plato, the narrator of the last conversation of Socrates.

THE CYNICS.

According to Zeller, the Cynical school was like the Megarian, a blending of Socratic philosophy with Eleatic and Sophistic doctrines, the two uniting in Stilpo, and going over into Stoicism with Zeno, who was one of Stilpo's disciples. Antisthenes, the founder of Cynicism, was in early life a disciple of Gorgias, and himself gave instruction in the art of rhetoric and the doctrines of the Sophists. Later, he became attached to Socrates, and was one of his most enthusiastic adherents. He taught in a gymnasium called Cynosarges, and appears to have been a man of high moral character, though Plato and Aristotle speak of his culture as superficial.

He recognized virtue as the supreme aim of life, and thought all knowledge useless that did not serve ethical aims. Virtue needs nothing except the strength of character of Socrates; it can do without theories and principles. The good is beautiful, the bad is ugly. The wise man is sufficient to himself; he possesses everything which others only seem to possess,

His own virtue makes him happy; he is at home everywhere in the world. Happiness is the final aim, but happiness and virtue are one. There is no good except virtue, no evil except vice. He alone is happy who is independent of externals, who desires nothing outside of that which is absolutely within his control. He must be lifted above poverty and riches, honor and shame, life and death, must fear nobody and care for nothing. He must be indifferent to all that concerns the public life of society and the private life of home; his feelings must be deadened to insensibility; he must renounce enjoyment itself, and find supreme self-satisfaction in virtue only.

The freedom of the Cynics is abstract and negative. True freedom consists in the control of one's needs and desires, not in their complete denial. Nor is it the highest morality to withdraw from human duties and relations, from participation in the life and interests of our fellow-men.

One may admire the force of will with which the Cynics pursued their aim, though it led to spiritual vanity and pride, rather than to Socratic elevation of character. They regarded themselves as physicians, able to heal the moral sickness of men, most of whom were fools enslaved by their desires. They occupied a peculiar position in the Greek world, and have been called the Capuchins of antiquity. In spite of their strangeness and extravagance, their influence was in part beneficial. They are said to have worn a distinctive dress, ragged and dirty, which did not escape the criticism of Socrates, to whom Antisthenes displayed the holes in his garment. "Ah," said Socrates, "through the hole itself I see your vanity."

Diogenes, of Sinope, was a disciple of Antisthenes, whose theories he exaggerated to the point of absurdity. "To have no needs," said Diogenes, "is divine; to have as few as possible comes nearest the divine." He threw away his cup as useless when he saw a boy drinking out of the palm of his hand. He once entered the dwelling of Plato, and walked around with dirty feet upon a beautiful carpet, saying, "Thus I trample on the pride of Plato." "Yes, but with a pride as great," replied Plato calmly.

The requirements of Cynicism were too severe to attract many disciples. It was incapable of scientific development. Its practical activity was of a negative kind, demanding renunciation and the separation of the individual from society. Man was to rely simply on his single self isolated from all other human selves, thus opening the way to vanity and pride and arbitrariness. "Cynicism thus touched its diametrical opposite—Hedonism," says Zeller.

THE CYRENAIC SCHOOL.

Aristippus of Cyrene, the founder of the Cyrenaic or Hedonic school, was a disciple of Socrates, though he is represented by Aristotle as a Sophist. He appears to have been a man of considerable culture when he first met Socrates. Brought up in the midst of wealth and luxury, his pleasure-loving habits contrasted strangely with the simplicity of his master. Of all the Socratists he was the first to require pay for his instructions, and himself sent money to Socrates, which was promptly returned.

Aristippus agrees with Antisthenes that happiness is the aim of philosophy, but he understands by happiness pleasure, the enjoyment of the moment. Only the present is ours, we must cease to concern ourselves with the past and the future; we can no longer possess the one and may never possess the other. Pleasure is a sensation of gentle motion: pain, of violent motion; the mean between the two is indifference. Pleasure is alone worthy of desire; quiet is mere insensibility like that of sleep. But insight is needed that we may choose and discriminate between our various appetites and desires; pleasure is sometimes bought at the expense of great pain.

The Cyrenaics, like the Epicureans, are forced to consider the results of actions, and soon discover that there are pleasures of the mind that outweigh in value those of the body. Mere satisfaction of the sensuous desires will not produce happiness; insight must be added, and the right mental disposition. Life offers the most to him who renounces no enjoyment, but remains at every instant master of himself.

Aristippus led a life of self-enjoyment, preserving his serenity under all circumstances. He knew how to use men and things for his own advantage, and made it his principle to free himself as far as possible from all sources of annoyance and trouble. He repels us by his superficial morality, and at the same time attracts us by his rare equanimity and moderation, which were purely Socratic.

His principle is one that contradicts itself. He declares that to be happy man must surrender himself with the full freedom of consciousness to the enjoyment of the present moment. But that freedom can only be attained by an elevation above immediate conditions and feelings. He bids us take no thought of the past or the future, and yet recommends insight and a consideration of the results of actions. Though he believes that pleasure is fixed by nature as man's ultimate aim, he sees that the aim is defeated unless it is controlled by prudential motives.

It is said that his grandson, Aristippus the younger, first systematized the doctrine of Hedonism. Other leaders of the school were Hegesias, Theodorus, and Anniceris.

Hedonism, Epicureanism, Eudæmonism and Utilitarianism, agree in considering man chiefly on the side of his sensations, as a being susceptible of pleasure and pain, whose proper pursuit is happiness. Opposite schools of morality, like the Cynics and Stoics, regard man almost exclusively on the side of his thoughts, as a being endowed with reason, self-consciousness, whose proper pursuit is virtue, the perfecting of his higher nature. The two ends usually harmonize, but when they conflict the question arises: Must we strive after the right or the useful, the just or the expedient? It is certain that Socrates answered the question in favor of right and justice, whatever Eudæmonistic interpretation may be placed on his theories. He was so many-sided that he was the source of fruitful impulses in widely different directions, while at the same time his thought was so imperfectly systematized as to be easily misunderstood and misapplied.

There is much in the doctrine of the Megarians, of the Cynics, and of the Cyrenaics, that is Sophistic rather than Socratic. But it is nevertheless clear that the three schools proceeded from Socrates as their starting point, and were necessary in order to bring to light all the consequences of the Socratic principles. Their scientific achievements were slight, but they were not without influence on the thought of Plato and Aristotle, and on the later course of philosophy.

Cynicism anticipated Stoicism; Cyrenaicism anticipated Epicureanism. But Plato is the complete Socratist, comprehending and working out the thought of his master, developing its rich content, and adding to it his own invaluable contributions.

CHAPTER XVIII.

PLATO'S LIFE AND WRITINGS.

THERE is no ancient philosopher with whose life we are more intimately acquainted than with that of Plato, yet even in his case authorities vary. He was born in the year 429 B.C., at the beginning of the Peloponnesian war, the year in which Pericles died. His father, Ariston, was a descendant of Codrus, the last hero-king of Attica; his mother, Perictione, was a descendant of Solon. His mother's uncle was the famous Kritias, the most talented and the most dangerous of the thirty tyrants of Athens.

Born of this illustrious race and favored by wealth, Plato must have found in his surroundings abundant means for the highest culture attainable in Athens. He received instruction from the most famous Sophists, and one of his teachers gave him the name that he has made illustrious—Plato; he was called by his family Aristokles. Some ascribe the name to the breadth of his forehead, others to the breadth of his mind and the wealth of his discourse. In his youth he cultivated poetry and wrote tragedies, dithyrambs and songs. In an epigram on Aster, one of his best friends, is a thought that reminds one of Romeo and Juliet:

> "To the stars thou look'st, my Aster,
> O, would that I were the heavens,
> So that I could see thee with so many eyes!"

In his twentieth year Plato made the acquaintance of Socrates, and during the long and confidential intercourse that followed, penetrated so deeply into the spirit of his master as to create for us his living portrait set in a frame of ideal beauty. The night before they met Socrates dreamed that a swan, the bird of Apollo, flew towards him with a melodious song, nestled in his breast, and then soared upward to heaven. Plato appreciated the debt he owed to Socrates and regarded it as the highest favor of fortune that he should have been born in his lifetime. His imaginative nature needed the logical discipline to which Socrates subjected his disciples, and it was, doubtless, this training that converted the poet into the philosopher. But the poet in Plato was never wholly lost; truth for him was ever one with beauty. It is probable that, at this time or earlier, Plato studied the systems of other philosophers. Aristotle says that he had been initiated into the Heraclitic doctrines by Cratylus before he met Socrates.

The tragic fate of his master must have been a heavy blow to Plato, and could not but deepen his reverence for the character and the principles that met even the ordeal of death unmoved. If, before this time, he had been reluctant to enter political life it is not strange that after the condemnation of Socrates he should renounce it entirely. The Athenian state appeared to him hopelessly inefficient, and it is well for humanity that he did not sacrifice himself in its ruin, but fled for refuge and strength to a higher, supersensuous world,—the world of Ideas.

After the execution of Socrates, Plato left Athens,

and took up his abode for a time at Megara, with his friend Euclid, the founder of the Megarian School of philosophy. He afterwards traveled to Kyrene, Egypt, Magna Græcia and Sicily. It is impossible to ascertain with certainty how long he remained in Megara, or whether he returned to Athens and taught philosophy, before completing what Schwegler terms his "*Wanderjahre.*" He gained from his travels a closer acquaintance with the Pythagorean school of philosophy, and a deeper knowledge of mathematics, which he studied under the guidance of the most celebrated mathematicians of the time. Zeller and other authorities regard as legendary the stories that are told of his stay in Egypt, and of the priestly lore and mysteries into which he was there initiated.

In Sicily, Plato visited the court of Dionysius the elder, whose youthful brother-in-law, Dion, embraced his doctrines. But the philosopher's plain speaking did not please Dionysius. Offended at his declaration that happiness is not dependent on external circumstances, he sent the philosopher to be sold in the slave-market of Ægina. The accounts of the affair vary, but Plato is said to have been ransomed by Anniceris, a Cyrenian. Dion and other friends, as the story goes, wished to repay the price of the ransom, but Anniceris refused the money for himself, and applied it to the purchase of the garden in the Academy. Here Plato gathered a chosen circle of disciples whom he instructed in philosophy. Among his auditors were two women. The Academy was a grove in the suburbs of Athens, used as a gymnasium, and named in honor of the hero

Academus, whose fame is entirely eclipsed by that of Plato.

Concerning the manner of his instruction we know little except what may be inferred from the form of his writings, and the decided way in which he condemns the long speeches of the rhetoricians, who know neither how to ask nor to answer questions. His discourses were doubtless conversational in character, although according to Aristotle he seems also to have delivered connected lectures, where the nature of the exposition rendered it necessary.

On the death of the elder Dionysius, Plato again visited Sicily, influenced by his friendship for Dion and the hope that he might effect a reform in the Sicilian constitution by winning over to his political views the heir of the throne, the younger Dionysius. Dionysius received Plato politely; but the philosopher's expectations were disappointed, for the young man had "one of those mediocre natures who in a half-hearted way strive for fame and distinction, but are capable of no depth and no earnestness." A quarrel breaking out between Dionysius and Dion which led to the banishment of the latter, Plato returned to Athens.

Some years afterward, moved by the solicitations of Dionysius and the entreaties of his friends, he made a third voyage to Sicily, hoping to effect a reconciliation between Dionysius and Dion. He not only failed in the attempt, but was so mistrusted by the tyrant that his life was endangered, and was saved only at the intercession of the Pythagoreans, then at the head of the Tarentine state.

It is said that Plato refused offers from various Greek states to become their lawgiver. It was a time when they did not prosper with their constitutions. But constitutions to be effective must be the outgrowth of historical conditions rather than the creation of individuals.

Honored everywhere, especially in Athens, Plato died on his birthday, in his 81st year, at a marriage feast. He was buried in the Ceramicus, not far from the Academy.

Plato lived at a time when Greece had reached her highest point of splendor, and was steadily declining in national greatness. His own nature and the influence of the time led him to philosophy rather than politics. His personality was more aristocratic than that of Socrates. Endowed with artistic tastes and the Greek love of beauty, he was not free from wants and desires, nor indifferent to the externals of life. But he always practiced the simplicity and moderation which he inculcated in his philosophy. He was exclusive in his friendships and did not seek to share his thoughts with all; he loved rather to shut out the world with its disturbing clamor. The aristocracy of intelligence, advocated in his ideal State, is deeply rooted in his own character. He united lofty moral principles with a rare susceptibility for beauty, grandeur of intellect with tenderness of feeling, enthusiasm with serenity, developing himself on all sides harmoniously, in accordance with the Greek ideal of human perfection.

"Plato's relation to the world is that of a superior spirit," says Goethe, "whose good pleasure it is to dwell in it for a time. It is not so much his concern to become acquainted with it—for the world and its nature are things which he presupposes—as to kindly communicate to it that which he brings with him, and of which it stands in great need. He penetrates into its depths, more that he may replenish them from the fullness of his own nature, than that he may fathom their mysteries. He scales its heights as one yearning after renewed participation in the source of his being. All that he utters has reference to something eternally complete, good, true, beautiful, whose furtherance he strives to promote in every bosom."

Like Pythagoras, he has been compared to Apollo, who in the bright clearness of his spirit was to the Greeks the very type of moral beauty, perfection and harmony.

His literary activity extended over the greater part of his life, and it is thought that none of his writings intended for publicity have been lost. Doubts have been thrown upon the genuineness of some of the minor Dialogues, but the authenticity of the greater ones is placed beyond dispute by the testimony of Aristotle. It is impossible to determine with certainty the dates of the several writings, a point that might help us towards comprehending the historical development of Plato's system of philosophy.

Schleiermacher classified the Dialogues according to an internal principle of connection, believing that Plato so planned his inquiries as to produce upon the reader's mind a certain effect, which would be presupposed in the succeeding investigation. He distinguished three divisions united in one organic whole; the elementary, the indirectly inquiring, and the expository or constructive dialogues.

Hermann agrees with Schleiermacher as to the unity of the writings, but finds its cause in the growth of Plato's mind rather than in any conscious design. He also arranges the Dialogues in three classes. The first is the Socratic elementary class, written before or immediately after the death of Socrates, dramatic in style and full of specious arguments, but penetrating no deeper than Socrates into the fundamental problems of thought. The second is the dialectic or mediatory class, written under the influence of the Megaro-Eleatic philosophy, distinguished by more searching criticism and less beauty of form. The third is the expository or constructive class, uniting the artistic fullness of the first with the philosophic profundity of the second, enriched by all the elements of an enlarged experience, and fused together into one perfect creation.

Hegel ascribes little importance to these inquiries, believing that it is only ignorance of philosophy that renders the apprehension of Plato's thought difficult. His system exhibits a totality of the Idea, in which the one-sided abstractions of earlier philosophers taken up into his deeper principle attain concrete unity and truth. For the concrete, according to Hegel, is the unity of different principles, each one of which must be set up as the sole truth in order to be developed and clearly conceived.

CHAPTER XIX.

CHARACTER OF PLATO'S PHILOSOPHY.

PLATO'S view concerning philosophy rests on a Socratic basis, but he goes far beyond his master in working out and perfecting his system of thought. With Plato as with Socrates, right action and right thinking are one; philosophy is inseparably connected with morality and religion. But it was Plato who first developed into a systematic whole the ethical concepts of Socrates, and found not only their basis but a guide for the explanation of the natural universe in dialectic, or the pure science of Ideas. That there is a difference as well as a connection between knowledge and action, was not wholly unobserved by Plato, although it was Aristotle who first clearly analyzed both, and distinguished beneath all apparent contradictions an essential identity in the activity of thought itself.

Plato, like Aristotle, entered upon physical investigations, which had been entirely neglected by Socrates. But Plato's achievements in this field are slight; to him the contemplation of pure ideas was far more important than the study of empirical data in the world of sense. For he regarded material things as types of eternal ideas, a world of shadows to be left behind if we would gain spiritual insight. He gladly turned from the transient appearance to its underlying reality, from the infinite in its finite manifestations to its revelation in pure thought.

Plato was the first Greek philosopher who studied the doctrines of his predecessors, and consciously united in a higher principle the truth of their contradictory statements. "The Socratic philosophy of concepts was transplanted by him into the fruitful and well-tilled soil of the previous natural philosophy," says Zeller, "thence to appropriate to itself all kindred matter; and in thus permeating the older speculation with the spirit of Socrates, purifying and refining it by dialectic, which was itself extended to metaphysical speculation; in thus perfecting ethics by natural philosophy and natural philosophy by ethics, Plato has accomplished one of the greatest intellectual creations ever known." He has proclaimed with energy and enthusiasm the deepest principle of all speculation, the idealism of thought, and given an impulse to the progress of philosophy, transcending far the bounds of his own system.

The form of the Platonic exposition, as is well known, is unique, and required an artistic nature for its construction. It is that of the philosophic dialogue, which retains the reciprocal kindling of thought peculiar to verbal intercourse, guided by a scientific purpose rather than contingent motives. Everything is simple and plastic. We are taken to the halls of the Gymnasia, or to the Academy, or to a banquet, or to the clear waters of the Ilyssus, where Socrates and other cultivated men are conversing. Each concedes to the other a perfect right to hold and to utter personal sentiments and opinions, which is the secret of that delightful Greek urbanity whose charm we all acknowledge. Socrates is the chief speaker and his personality, idealized by Plato, is the bond of artistic unity between the dialogues. Plato realized that he owed the beautiful fruit of his thought to the seed that Socrates so generously scattered, and his writings are one grateful acknowledgment to the revered and beloved master.

It is not difficult to distinguish in the dialogue what belongs to Plato and what belongs to Socrates; for philosophy is one, and later systems of thought can only develop the truth implicitly contained in the earlier. Plato's creative genius is shown by the manner in which he uses his intellectual material, original and inherited, forming it into a plastic whole as beautiful and complete as a work of Phidias. Thought to him is a conversation of the soul with itself, and the form of the dialogue is essentially connected with his idea of philosophy. He had a deep conviction of the advantages of speech as compared with writing, and sought by his peculiar method to compel the reader to an active participation in philosophic inquiries. He first arouses interest in the different opinions expressed by various speakers, and then, after a rigid analysis and investigation which exhibits their incompleteness, leaves the reader to discover for himself the central point of unity in the argument. The unfolding of the dialogue is in fact the development of a philosophic theme. The speakers not only give their opinions, but fill the parts prescribed for them by the author. Many of the questions of Socrates are so framed that a simple yes or no, is all the answer required; but, with few exceptions, the art is so perfect as to preserve the life and spirit of a real conversation.

Philosophy to Plato was not a mere doctrine, but a living power which he sought to communicate to others through actual personal communion, or the written speech that resembled it most nearly. The philosophic dialogue is as much his creation and peculiarity as the system of thought it embodies, and could never have reached equal perfection earlier or later. Philosophy demanded a sharper discrimination between the æsthetic impulse and scientific cognition, and renounced the plastic beauty of Plato's style for a more systematic exposition of its principles in the works of Aristotle.

The employment of myths is another peculiarity of Plato's philosophy. The myth is an exposition by means of sensuous pictures addressed to imagination and feeling rather than to the pure thinking activity. It is a poetic presentment of that which the author believes to be true, but cannot prove scientifically. Like all symbolic representation, it is necessarily obscure and ambiguous. To interpret it strictly would be the task, and not a very enviable one, of some person who had plenty of time on his hands, says Plato in the Phaedo. Too much or too little is frequently found in it; its hidden meaning is either extended to utterly foreign subjects or lost sight of entirely. It was the poet in Plato that clothed the myth in such mystic radiance, but its use was a necessity to the philosopher. He could not otherwise fill up the gaps in scientific knowledge that existed in his day, or express those higher realities of religion and faith which transcend human experience.

But, from a scientific point of view, Plato's use of the myth is a sign of weakness rather than of strength. The idea clothed in a sensuous form is neither fully comprehended nor expressed. Plato, like a creative artist, thinks in pictures and sees the truth intuitively; but this is poetry rather than philosophy. Philosophy must confine itself strictly to the domain of the pure intellect, and leave to poetry that of the imagination.

Plato himself, in distinguishing between the different grades of knowing, placed the truth in that alone which is produced through thought. In opposition to the view of ordinary consciousness and that of the Sophists, he teaches that knowledge is neither perception nor correct opinion, but the activity of the soul itself in the sphere of ideas. If perception were knowledge, that would be true for each man which appears to him true; if correct opinion were knowledge, there would be no possibility of false opinion, for we can only know or not know. Opinion is intermediate between knowledge and ignorance, and is uncertain and variable because it lacks insight into the necessity of truth.

Passing from the theoretical to the practical, Plato teaches that the virtue which is guided by opinion is dependent on chance, and circumstances, and the subjective will of the individual. But virtue in its essence is immutable, and is based upon knowledge. Against the view of the Sophists, who consider pleasure the highest good, Plato argues that the good can only be the just, that it is better to suffer wrong than to do it, to be punished for evil than to remain unpunished. "The philosopher only has true happiness," he says, "for his pleasure alone consists in being filled with something real; that is the sole pleasure which is unalloyed and bound to no conditioning pain. The question whether justice is more profitable than injustice is as absurd as would be the inquiry, 'Is it better to be sick or well?'"

Philosophy, according to Plato, is derived from practical necessity, and springs from inspiration or enthusiasm, the philosophic *Eros*. This enthusiasm assumes the form of love on account of the special brightness which distinguishes the visible copies of the beautiful. The soul, through love, seeks to fill itself with what is eternal and imperishable. Love is the striving of mortal nature after immortality. It does not at first reveal its true nature, but rises gradually from the love of beautiful forms to the love of beautiful souls, and finally to the love of that which is its true goal—the Divine Idea, or Beauty in Eternal Existence. Love, as conceived by Plato, is the philosophic impulse which seeks, through speculative knowledge and the practice of virtue, to expand the finite to infinity.

When we ask how love is to obtain its highest object of endeavor, Plato unexpectedly supplements love by logic, and adds to the philosophic impulse a severe training in the dialectic method. "Enthusiasm is the first irregular production of ideas," says

Hegel, "but it is scientific thought that brings them into a rationally developed shape and into the daylight." Plato declares that dialectic is the true fire of Prometheus, the instrument by means of which the pure idea is developed. It is a recognition of the essence of things, of the One in the Many, and the Many in the One. It proves that the only reality is spirit, and that thought is the truth of the sensuous world.

Through the union of love and logic, of the dialectic impulse and the philosophic method, Plato develops his philosophy. The highest object of thought is the Idea of the Good, and the chief problem of education is to incline the soul towards this Idea. In a brilliant allegory Plato represents men as dwelling underground, in a cave, with a long entrance open towards the light. At a distance above and behind them a fire is blazing, but they are fastened in such a manner that they cannot turn their heads, and can only see the shadows cast by those who pass along a raised way between them and the fire. They look upon these shadows as realities; and if one is freed and dragged toward the fire, or upward into the full blaze of the sun, he is filled with pain and terror, and blinded by excess of light. But he will come at last to recognize the truth, and will see that what he now beholds is the substance of the shadow. Should he descend again into the darkness of the cave, he will not see as well as his companions, and will be mocked as one who went on a visit to the sun and lost his eyes. But the way into the light is the way to knowledge, and those who attain to the beatific vision of the Idea of the Good are always going upward. The soul must be turned away from the transient occurrences surrounding it until it is able to contemplate true existence. This is the meaning of education; it is a knowing from within, and not from without. He alone is capable of philosophic cognition who has learned to renounce the sensuous, and to direct his vision towards true Being.

Philosophy, to Plato, is the royal science that all others must serve, the realization and perfection of human nature, the absolute consummation of the spiritual life. "The knowledge of the most excellent things begins through the eyes," he says in the Timaeus. "The distinction of the visible day from the night, the lunations and revolutions of the planets, have produced the knowledge of time and given rise to the investigation of the nature of the whole. Whence we have gained philosophy; and a greater good than it, given by God to man, has neither come nor will ever come."

Plato recognizes that God alone is wise, and does not claim for man divinity, but only its likeness. He acknowledges that it is difficult for the human soul amid its earthly surroundings to attain the pure intuition of truth, but sees in self-activity the means of development. He would even base the organism of the state on philosophy. "Until philosophers rule in the state, or the now so-called kings and men in power philosophize truly and perfectly, and thus the ruling power and philosophy coincide — until the different dispositions are united which now are isolated, and engaged in these provinces separately for themselves, pursuing the one or the other; until then, oh friend Glaucon, there will be no end of evil for the people, nor, think I, for the human race in general." Plato's thought, so far as it means that universal principles should direct and control the state, is true, and is generally acknowledged to-day as the substantial basis of government.

"Plato has indicated every eminent point in speculation," says Emerson. "He wrote on the scale of the mind itself, so that all things have symmetry in his tablet. He put in all the past without weariness, and descended into detail with a courage like that he witnessed in nature. One would say that his forerunners had mapped out each a farm, or a district, or an island, in intellectual geography, and that Plato first drew the sphere. He domesticates the soul in nature; man is the microcosm. All the circles of the visible heaven represent as many circles in the rational soul. There is no lawless particle, and there is nothing casual in the action of the human mind. * * * * Before all men he saw the intellectual values of the moral sentiment. He describes his own ideal when he paints in the Timæus a god leading things out of disorder into order. He kindled a fire so truly in the centre that we see the sphere illuminated, and can distinguish poles, equator, and lines of latitude, every arc and every node; a theory so arranged, so modulated that you would say the winds of ages had swept through this rhythmic structure, and not that it was the brief extempore blotting of one short-lived scribe. * * * His subtlety commended him to men of thought. The secret of his popular success is the moral aim, which endeared him to mankind. Intellect, he said, is king of heaven and earth; but in Plato, intellect is always moral."

CHAPTER XX.

THE PLATONIC DIALECTIC.

THE division of philosophy into dialectic, physics, and ethics, is that which is generally adopted in the exposition of the Platonic system. This classification cannot be distinctly ascribed to Plato himself, but is one presupposed by Aristotle, and employed by Plato's disciple, Xenocrates.

Dialectic, in the higher sense of the word, is the science of true Being, the inquiry into Ideas. The Idea for Plato is the true Universal, the essence of things, that which abides uniform and self-identical amid all finite changes and contradictions. It is apprehended, not by the senses, but by reason alone. All that the senses perceive is constantly changing, becoming; no single thing exists truly, for it depends on another, and is self-contradictory; the true is not the sensible, but the intelligible world. "There are two sorts of things," says the Timæus, "one that always is and becomes not, and one that always becomes and never is. The former, that, namely, which is always in the same state, is apprehended through reflection by means of reason; the other, again, which comes to be and ceases to be, but properly never is, is apprehended through opinion by means of sensuous perception and without reason." One is the archetypal Idea ; the the other is its imperfect copy. We are led to the first when we look for the ultimate end of the second; that which is fair and good in the finite world can only become so through participation in Infinite Beauty and Goodness. Everything points to the idea as the cause of its existence; the Ideal is the only Real. This particular rose, with its bloom and fragrance, is a transitory image of the universal rose that never fades.

Hegel distinguishes between the higher form of dialectic employed by Plato, and that which he used in common with Socrates and the Sophists. In some of the dialogues, dialectic is apparently an art of overturning the common notions of men by showing what contradictions they contain and how inadequate they are as scientific knowledge. Its purpose is to direct men to search for what *is* instead of what *appears*; but its result is negative and destructive. That Plato appreciated the danger involved in this use of dialectic is evident from the advice given in the Republic, that citizens should not be initiated into the art before they had completed their thirtieth year. But there is a positive side even to this form of dialectic. It classifies under one general view the notions analyzed, and thus brings to consciousness the Universal. Plato seems a little tedious to modern thought in this procedure because the abstractions at which he arrives are part of our intellectual inheritance.

"The dialectic as speculative is the Platonic dialectic proper," says Hegel: "it does not end with a negative result, but presents the union of antithetic sides which have annulled each other. What Plato seeks in the dialectic is the pure thought of the reason, from which he very carefully discriminates the understanding. One can have thought concerning many things, if he has thought at all; but Plato does not mean this sort of thoughts. The true speculative greatness of Plato, that through which he makes an epoch in the history of philosophy, and consequently in the world-history in general, is the more definite comprehension of the Idea; an insight which some centuries later constitutes the fundamental element in the formation of the world-history and in the new organic form of the human spirit."

Plato's dialectic starts from that of Socrates, but he unites in his thought all the principles of the earlier philosophers, dissolving their contradictions by means of that higher insight into truth contained in his theory of Ideas. He derives from Heraclitus the doctrine that sensuous things are perpetually changing; to the Eleatics he owes the conception of absolute Being; from Socrates he learns to seek the universal in the determination of concepts, and comes to the conclusion, as Aristotle says, that "this procedure must refer to something different from sense, for sensible things, being always liable to change, cannot be universally defined." That which exists absolutely, and is alone the object of knowledge, he calls Ideas. The sensuous manifold that we perceive is what it is by virtue of participation in Ideas. The visible is but an adumbration of the invisible; sense reflects imperfectly the reality of thought. Ideas are the eternal prototypes of Being; from them all other things are copied. They belong to the spiritual and not to the material world; they are accessible to the contemplation of reason alone, and can neither be seen nor apprehended by sense and understanding.

In the Symposium, Plato defines the Idea of the Beautiful, and shows how one may be guided from the love of its imperfect copies in the world of sense, on and on, with increasing apprehension of the truth until, at last, purified of earthly leaven, he sees what the essence of Beauty is, and beholds its divine Idea, the Infinite Cause of all that is fair and lovely in earth or heaven. "But what if man had eyes to see the true beauty—the divine beauty, I mean, pure and clear and unalloyed, not clogged with the pollutions of mortality, and all the colors and vanities of human life — thither looking, and holding converse with the true beauty, divine and simple, and bringing into being and educating true creations of virtue and not idols only? Do you not see that in that communion only, beholding beauty with the eye of the mind, he will be enabled to bring forth, not images of beauty, but realities; for he has hold not of an image but of a reality, and bringing forth and educating true virtue to become the friend of God and be immortal, if mortal man may?"

Ideas are present in the mind of every individual, but few are aware of their existence, or know anything of their nature and character. The special function of dialectic is to make us conscious of their presence, and to purify our thinking by directing it towards the true aim of human activity, the spiritual rather than the material. Education is not only useful information, but an illumination and purification of the soul. In the seventh Book of the Republic, Plato explains the nature of dialectic and the training that is necessary to draw the soul upwards. Arithmetic and geography prepare the mind for true science by teaching it how to deal with abstractions apart from sensible objects. Yet mathematics is but a dream and a hypothesis, never analyzing its own principles in order to attain true knowledge. Dialectic, and dialectic alone, is the only science which does away with hypotheses in order to establish them, and teaches the eye of the soul, buried in the slough of ignorance, to look upwards, using as handmaids the other sciences. Dialectic may be further defined as the science which explains the essence of each thing, which distinguishes and abstracts the conception of the Good, and is ready to disprove all objections, not by appeals to opinion, but to true existence. This is the knowledge without which man apprehends only shadows, and dreaming and slumbering in this life reaches its end before he is well awake.

To become conscious that one cannot think a sensation without passing beyond it to the idea that lies at its basis, is a discovery that summons the human intellect to put forth its utmost capacities. To think is to pass from the singular and particular to the idea or the universal. Before me lie a rose and a lily, and I apprehend that each is like and unlike the other. But whence comes this apprehension? Can resemblance or difference be seen, or touched, or perceived by any of the senses? Are they not universal relations which can only be apprehended by the intellect? Are they not laws of thought without which intelligence could not operate? Can we think at all except under the conditions of resemblance and difference, of genus and species? Can we know anything of a world that is not constructed in conformity with these ideas? Are not the laws of thought objective as well as subjective, universal, necessary?

Absolute and universal truth, according to Plato, must address itself to all intellect, and he therefore argues that ideas are the truest realities because they are the principles without which there could be neither intelligence nor the object of intelligence. The world of thought is the actual world itself; it alone exists truly and is capable of being known. It does not lie outside of reality, it is not beyond in heaven or elsewhere, it is here and now, eternal and divine in its nature. To become conscious of its presence we have only to develop our inner capacities, to see with the eye of the mind. "Ideas are to be reached only in and through scientific cognition," says Hegel, "they are immediate intuitions only in so far as they consist of the simple results which scientific cognition arrives at by its processes."

Science, the knowledge of that which is in truth,

is therefore distinguished from opinion. Plato, in the Republic, says that opinion is the middle ground between ignorance and knowledge, and that its content is a mingling of Being and Nought. The subject matter of opinion is the world of sensuous objects, the individual thought which at the same time is and is not, since it only participates in ideas and reflects them imperfectly. Can we say of any finite thing that it is absolutely large or small, light or heavy? It is not merely one of these opposites but the other, as, for instance, in the Phædo, Simmias is large in comparison with Socrates, small in comparison with Phædo. But the idea of largeness remains what it is permanently, and is never at the same time identical with smallness. Only the idea can be known; for of thought which is constantly changing, we may have opinion but not knowledge. Opinion refers to the material, knowledge to the immaterial. To assume that the two are identical is to become a materialist; to distinguish between them is to acknowledge the existence of Ideas, unchangeable and imperishable.

The nature of knowledge, as opposed to perception, is considered at length in the Theætetus. The definition that "Knowledge is sensible perception," is first analyzed. This is soon identified with the saying of Protogoras that "Man is the measure of all things." "Things are to me as they appear to me and to you as they appear to you." Suppose the same wind blowing in our faces: it is hot or cold, according to your feeling, or to mine. Feeling, perception, appearance, are identical with being and knowledge. But if truth is only sensation and one man's discernment is as good as another's, and every man is his own judge, and everything that he judges is right and true, why should we go for instruction to Protagoras, or know less than he, or refuse to believe the contradictory proposition, that every man is not the measure of all things? What need of discussion, or debate, or scientific inquiry, if subjective feeling is the criterion of knowledge? Would not Protagoras have to contradict himself and admit the truth of what his opponents advance, if every man perceives and feels correctly? How could there be any difference in the judgments of men about the future? Yet we admit practically that only the wise man knows what is expedient for the future. The farmer is a better judge of the prospective harvest than the man who knows nothing of farming; Protagoras himself is a better judge of the probable effect of a speech than an indifferent person. Finally, if the objects of sensation are constantly moving and changing, as Protagoras asserts, how is it possible to fix them even for an instant? Is not perception itself annihilated? What can be predicted of that which is in a perpetual flux?

It has been objected that Plato is not wholly fair to Protagoras and interprets him one-sidedly. But the truth remains, that knowledge is not sensible perception, or in Plato's words, "Knowledge does not consist in impressions of sense, but in reasoning about them; in that only, and not in the mere impression, truth and being can be attained." "We cannot apprehend either through hearing or through sight that which they have in common. To compare one sensation with another implies a principle which is above sensation. To combine perceptions in the unity of self-consciousness is a purely intellectual act. Through what organ of the body would one perceive mathematical and other abstractions, unity and multiplicity, sameness and difference, likeness and unlikeness, and the most universal of all, being? We know a thing to be hard or soft by the touch, but the essential being of hardness or softness, their opposition to one another and the nature of the opposition, is slowly learned by reflection and experience.

Knowledge, then, is not perception, and must be sought elsewhere. Is it correct opinion? The Greek word for opinion (δοχα), like the German *Meinung* and *Vorstellung*, is difficult to translate. It is used in various senses by Plato, and is explained by one commentator as crude conception, feeling, instinctive conviction. But these terms do not exhaust its meaning, as is evident from the following passage: "The soul when thinking appears to me to be just talking—asking questions of herself, and answering them, affirming and denying. And when she has arrived at a decision, either gradually or by a sudden impulse, and has at last agreed, and does not doubt, this is called her opinion." Plato proves that opinion is not knowledge, and the dialogue ends without reaching the definition sought. The light thrown on the subject, though indirect, is none the less valuable.

The work begun in the Theætetus is continued in the Sophist, where Plato investigates the ideas of movement and rest, of Being and Non-Being. The

Sophist is an imaginary representative of false opinion. But falsehood is that which is not, and therefore has no existence. If we admit that falsehood exists, we presuppose the conception of Non-Being; "for only that opinion can be named false which asserts the non-existence of things which are, and the existence of things which are not." The same difficulty occurs if we define the Sophist as the imitator of appearance and not of reality. How can he imitate that which is not? The argument again asserts the existence of Non-Being, which is positively denied by Parmenides and the Eleatics.

Parmenides affirms that all things are one, that we cannot perceive the many because the many are not, that plurality and change, space and time, are merely illusions of the senses. Plato, on the other hand, seeks to establish the reality of Non-Being, explaining it as the other of Being, both of which belong to all things. Non-Being is negation, and is essential to any distinction. It becomes, as it were, positive in relation to that to which it is opposed. The not large is as real as the large, darkness is as real as light, cold as heat. In relation to itself light is, in relation to darkness, is not; to know what it is we must know what it is not; negation is as necessary as affirmation. True being contains difference as well as identity, being for others as well as for self. The being of the Eleatics is altogether exclusive; the being of Plato is altogether inclusive.

In opposition to the Eleatics, the Sophists hold fast to Non-Being, which is the standpoint of sensation, or the many. This view leads to materialism, to the belief of those who, according to Plato, "are dragging down all things from heaven and from the unseen to earth, and seem determined to grasp in their hands rocks and oaks; of these they lay hold and are obstinate in maintaining that the things only which can be touched or handled have being or essence, because they define being and body as one, and if any one says that what is not a body exists they altogether despise him and will hear of nothing but body." Plato represents their opponents as cautiously defending themselves from above out of an unseen world, mightily contending that true essence consists of certain intelligible and incorporeal ideas; the bodies which the materialists maintain to be the very truth they break up into little bits by arguments and affirm them to be generation and not essence. These "Friends of Ideas," as Plato terms them, assert that neither motion, nor life, nor soul, nor mind, are present with absolute Being, that to it belongs neither activity nor passivity.

Against this doctrine of "an everlasting fixture in awful unmeaningness," Plato argues forcibly that the Divine Reason could exist nowhere, nor in any one, if it were unmoved, and had neither life, nor soul, nor thought. If we are to participate in Being, we must act upon it or be acted upon by it; if we are to know Being, a capacity of being known must correspond to our faculty of knowledge. It is as difficult to conceive Being as Non-Being if the two are held in utter isolation. Non-Being is the principle of the other which runs through all things. In spite of Parmenides who says, "Non-Being never is and do thou keep thy thoughts from this way of inquiry," Plato proves that "there is a communion of classes, and that being, and difference, or other, traverse all things, and mutually interpenetrate, so that the other partakes of being and is by reason of this participation, and yet is not that of which it partakes, but other, and being other than being, is clearly and manifestly not-being. And again, being, though partaking of the other, becomes a class other than the remaining classes, and being other than all of them, is not each one of them and is not all the rest, so that there are thousands and thousands of cases in which being is not as well as is, and all other things, whether regarded individually or collectively, in many respects are, and in many respects are not."

The concept of motion, for instance, excludes that of rest, but both participate in being. Each is identical with itself, but the other of the other. So far as concepts are alike, the being denoted by one belongs to the other; so far as they are different, the contrary is the case, and the being of one is the non-being of the other. The concept man, for instance, includes all those concepts which distinguish man as an animal, and those also which separate him from other animals, but it excludes an infinite number of concepts which are other and different from man. Thus in every being there is also a non-being, the difference. He is the master of dialectic who sees clearly the reciprocal relation of concepts, and knows what classes have and have not communion with one another. But he who is always bringing forward oppositions in argument is but a little way in the investigation of truth. The attempt at universal separation is the annihilation of reason, for thought consists in the uniting of ideas.

The identity of Being and Non-Being constitutes, according to Hegel, the true point of interest in Platonic philosophy. "As for the imagination," he says, "it is well enough to arouse it and animate it with representations of the Beautiful and the Good; but the thinking cognition asks after a definite statement regarding the nature of the Eternal and Divine. And the nature of this Eternal and Divine is, essentially, free determination alone, and the being determined does not in any way interfere with its universality; a limitation (for every determination is limitation) which nevertheless leaves the Universal in its infinitude free by itself. Freedom exists only in the return-into itself, the undistinguished is lifeless; the active, living, concrete universal is, therefore, that which distinguishes itself within itself, but remains free in the process. This determination consists only in this; that the one is self-identical in its Other, in the Many, in the Different."

The Parmenides, through a more abstract and elaborate dialectic, attains the same result as the Sophist. Parmenides is the chief speaker, and his conclusion that the one is not thinkable without the many, nor the many without the one, is opposed to the Eleatic doctrine. But Plato may have regarded his theory of ideas as a development of the Eleatic conception of being, and a conciliation of its contradictory elements. Parmenides certainly assails Plato's theory in the first part of his discourse, anticipating in the most wonderful way the criticism of after ages. Plato here touches on the deepest problem of philosophy, the connection between the Ideas in us and the Absolute Idea, between the human and the Divine.

Concerning the unity of the one and the many, Socrates says; "I should be surprised to hear that the genera and the species had opposite qualities in themselves; but if a person wanted to prove to me that I was many and one, there would be no marvel in that. When he wanted to show that I was many he would say that I have a right and a left side, and an upper and a lower half, for I cannot deny that I partake of multitude; when, on the other hand, he wants to prove that I am one, he will say that we who are here assembled are seven, and that I am one and partake of the one, and in saying both he speaks truly. · · · If, however, as I was suggesting just now, we have to make an abstraction, I mean of like, unlike, one, many, rest, motion, and similar ideas and then to show that these in their abstract form admit of admixture and separation, I should greatly wonder at that."

Parmenides admires the noble ardor with which the youthful Socrates pursues philosophy, not holding fast to the sensuous, but to concepts which are seized by thought alone. But he recommends Socrates to practice dialectic, and to consider not only what follows from assuming a determination, but what follows from assuming its opposite. This leads to the second and most important part of the dialogue, the dialectical treatment of the one and the many by Parmenides himself. It is first proved that the one that cannot be many is not even one, that it is "neither named nor uttered, nor conceived, nor known," and that the reality of the many apart from the one is also unthinkable. The hypothesis that the one is not is equally impossible to thought, and the conclusion is reached that "whether one is or is not, one and the other in relation to themselves or one another, all of them, in every way, are and are not, and appear and appear not."

"The One is the Totality—All that is—Being and Non-Being—One and Many," to quote the words of Mr. S. H. Emery, in his exposition of the Parmenides, published in the *Journal of Speculative Philosophy*. "The negative series of propositions contains the first negation of a negation," says Prof. Jowett. "Two minus signs in arithmetic or algebra make a plus. Two negations destroy each other. This subtle notion is the foundation of the Hegelian logic. The mind must not only admit that determination is negation, but must get through negation into affirmation. · · · That Plato and the most subtle philosopher of the nineteenth century should have lighted upon the same notion is a singular coincidence of ancient and modern thought."

True Being must be defined as a unity which includes in itself multiplicity. All things draw their existence from the one and the many, and contain the finite and the infinite as a part of their nature. The phenomenal world derives its reality from that which shines through it—Ideas. Plato does not deny, but explains actual existence. The plurality of the phenomenon is sustained and comprehended by the unity of the idea.

In the Philebus, Plato distinguishes four determinations of existence ; the infinite, or unlimited, the limited, the union of the two, and the cause of the union. To the cause he ascribes reason and wisdom ; it is the Divine Providence everywhere adapting means to ends ; the Absolute comprehending in itself the finite and the infinite. "The distinction of the absolute and relative forms the logical ground-work of Plato's whole system," says Zeller ; "for the idea exists in and for itself; the phenomenon, and to the fullest extent, matter, only in relation to something else."

In bridging the chasm between thought and sense, between ideas and phenomena, Plato is not always consistent with himself. At one time he describes the outward world as if it were mere subjective appearance ; at another, he demands that the meanest material existence shall not be left without an idea. He struggles against this dualism, but does not overcome it wholly. That the essence of things is the same as the divine essence, is implied in his speculations, although in the Timæus. as Hegel says, "the two appear distinct from each other—God, *And* the essence of things."

Plato also expressed the union of the one and the many by describing the ideas as numbers. That ideas are nothing but numbers is a view ascribed to Plato by Aristotle, but not found in the dialogues and therefore unsubstantiated.

The Platonic Ideas are so related as to form a graduated series and organism, combining, excluding, or participating in one another in all conceivable ways. The lower presuppose the higher, and the highest of all, without presupposition, is the Idea of the Good, which gives to everything whatever worth it possesses. As the sun in the visible world enlightens the eye and reveals things seen, everywhere causing growth and increase, so in the invisible world the Good is the source of truth and knowledge. It is represented as the goal of human activity, that which all men pursue under different names, the ultimate end of the world, the source of reality and reason. It is higher than the idea of Being; everything that is and is knowable has received from God its existence and its ability to be known. Plato clearly asserts in the Philebus that the Divine Reason is none other than the Good, and identifies it in the Timæus with the Creator and world-builder. He seems never to have separated in his thought God as a person from the Idea of the Good.

Plato identifies religion with philosophy; God in an absolute sense is not distinct from the highest of the Ideas. He recognizes the gods of the popular religion, but places above them One who is all-wise and all-powerful, creating the world because He is good and ruling it by the supremacy of His reason. From His goodness he deduces His unchangeableness; for that which is perfect can neither be changed by another nor alter in itself. God is wanting in nothing that is fair and excellent; He is able to do whatever can be done at all; His wisdom is seen in the perfect adaptation of means to ends; He is absolute goodness and justice. To worship God is to seek to be like Him, to create in ourselves His image. Philosophy is not mere abstract speculation, it is love and life, the filling of the soul with the true and the infinite.

Dialectic, the development of the method by which the truth is ascertained, is inseparably united with moral culture. Plato teaches us to open the inward eye and see that which is in reality, turning away the thought and inclination from the sensible to the intelligible. The discipline of dialectic is moral as well as intellectual; the highest insight which it enables us to attain is the object of religion as well as of philosophy—the Idea of God as Absolute Goodness.

CHAPTER XXI.

THE PLATONIC PHYSICS.

PLATO'S discussions concerning the world of phenomena, the Cosmos and man, are included under the name of Physics. But he tells us that in this field of investigation we must be content to take probability for our guide, and not look for the same accuracy of treatment as in dialectic. His themes are set forth in the Timæus, the most difficult and obscure of his dialogues, and the one most strongly colored with Pythagoreanism.

Nature, the world of phenomena, is that which is always becoming and never is; it is apprehended not by reason and reflection, but by opinion with the help of sense. As visible and tangible it must have been created; and that which is created must have a cause. This cause is the Father of all who looked to an eternal archetype, for the world is the fairest of creations, and God is the best of causes. He created the world because He was good, and desired that all things should be as like Himself as possible. He brought order out of disorder, and reflecting that of visible things the intelligent is superior to the unintelligent, He put intelligence in soul, and soul in body, and framed the universe to be the best and fairest work in the order of nature.

Thus, through the providence of God, the world became a living soul and truly rational. He created it before the body, compounding out of the unchangeable and indivisible essence and also out of the divisible and corporeal a third nature intermediate between them which partook of the same and the other. The whole was divided lengthwise, and the two halves were bent into an outer and an inner circle; the outer is the circle of the same, or the sphere of fixed stars; the inner is the circle of the other, which forms the seven spheres of the planets. In the circular revolution of these spheres the soul turning on itself moves, and at the same time moves the corporeal, interfused everywhere from the centre of the universe to the circumference. Its form, that of a sphere, is the most perfect and uniform of shapes, comprehending all others; and its motion is circular because, as return into itself, it is most appropriate to mind and intelligence. It is divided according to the cardinal numbers of the harmonic and astronomical systems, for numbers are the mean between mere sensuous existence and the pure idea, and the soul of the world must comprehend in itself all proportion and measure. The mythical element is at once apparent in this description. The immaterial is confused with the material; imagination seeks to picture that which cannot be pictured, but which can only be thought by the pure reason.

Plato believed the Cosmos to be a living creature with a soul. All that is moved by another must be preceded by the self-moved; the corporeal is moved by another, the soul is self-moved. If we regard the universe, it is impossible to doubt that it is ruled by intelligence, and where, except in the soul, can this intelligence dwell? The soul is therefore prior to the body, both in man and in the Cosmos. And as the body of the Cosmos is more glorious and mighty than ours, its soul transcends our soul in perfection. The soul of the world is the intermediate principle between the Idea and the phenomenon, participating in the Divine Reason and imparting it to the corporeal. It is not only the cause of material motion, but it is also the source of spiritual life and knowledge. Never growing old nor passing away, it is the perfect copy of the everlasting and invisible God, itself a blessed god exalted above all other created deities. "Even Plato is too deeply penetrated with the glory of nature to despise her as the non-divine," says Zeller, "or to rank her as the unspiritual, below human self-consciousness."

Hegel finds a profound meaning underlying Plato's doctrine of the world-soul. The nature of the Absolute Idea is shown in forming out of the undivided and the divided a mixture, partaking of the nature of the self-identical and of the other, and uniting all into one whole which is "the true matter, the absolute stuff (material) which is sundered in itself, as an abiding and indissoluble unity of one and many. Plato finds the soul to be the all-including simple in the idea of the corporeal universe;

to him the essence of the corporeal and of the soul is that of the Unity in the Difference. This twofold Essence, posited in and for itself in the Difference, systematizes itself within the One into many moments, which, however, are movements; so this reality and the mentioned essence are, taken together, the whole in the antithesis of soul and body, and the antithetic sides are again one. Spirit is the all-penetrating to which the corporeal is opposed, though the former (spirit) is, in fact, this extension itself."

The archetype of the world-soul exists alone in thought, in eternal self-identity; but entering into antithesis a copy arises and becomes visible. The archetype is the life eternal; the copy is the system of sidereal motion, a self-moving image of the eternal. Moved according to number it is what we call time. The true time is eternal, or the present. Every thought exists in time; like space, it is sensuous and not sensuous, the form in which spirit becomes objective. Opposite to true time, or the eternal present, the form of the self-identical, is that of the self-changing, the phenomenal world of matter. Space is its ideal essence, as time is the absolute principle of the immediate image of the Eternal.

That Plato believed matter to be eternal, independent, existing as chaos before the creation of the world, might be inferred from certain passages of the Timæus. But to interpret literally what was only meant figuratively would contradict other statements of a deeper philosophic import, and would place beside the Idea of the Good another entity, equally permanent and self-identical. Plato seems rather to conceive matter as the unlimited, the condition of separation and division, the objective which has the power of receiving the idea and reflecting it in the phenomenon. It is the ground of change and of extension, and must be different from the Idea, because it is that in which its copy exists.

Plato enters into details concerning the derivation of the four elements, and classifies animated beings accordingly into those of fire or light, of air, of water, and of earth. He describes the earth as at rest in the centre of the universe, and conceives the stars as immortal deities. His discussions concerning organic nature and the structure of the human body remind us that science was yet in its infancy. He distinguishes between two causes, the divine and the necessary. The divine appertains to the eternal, the necessary to the finite and mortal. God himself is the author of the first; but the second He commits to His assistants for the production and regulation of mortal things; "an easy mode of transition from the divine to the finite," says Hegel.

Plato's theory of the human soul is the completion of his physics. Conceived apart from its union with the body, the essence of the human soul is the same as that of the world-soul. Reason cannot impart itself to man except through its instrumentality; participating in the idea of life it can never participate in the opposite idea, that of death. It is self-moved and the source of motion in all other things; it is indestructible, without end or beginning, free from change and multiplicity. Its connection with matter is expressed mythically as a lapse to a lower condition. The soul is represented under the figure of two winged steeds and a charioteer. The white horse is the symbol of its higher aspirations, the black horse is the symbol of appetite and impulse, the charioteer is the reason. If perfect and fully winged it soars upward and regulates the world, if imperfect it droops and receives an earthly form, which appears to be self-moved, but is really moved by the soul. The immortal, according to Hegel's interpretation of Plato's thought, is that whose soul and body are indivisibly in one, the identity of the real and the ideal, of the finite and the infinite.

"Now the chariots of the gods, self-balanced, upward glide in obedience to the rein; but the others have a difficulty, for the steed who has evil in him, if he has not been properly trained by the charioteer, gravitates and inclines and sinks towards the earth: and this is the hour of agony and extremest conflict in the soul. For the immortal souls, when they are at the end of their course, go out and stand upon the back of heaven, and the revolution of the spheres carries them round and they behold the world beyond. * * * The colorless and formless and intangible essence is visible to the mind, which is the only lord of the soul. * * During the revolution she beholds justice, temperance, and knowledge absolute, not in the form of generation or of relation, which men call existence, but knowledge absolute in existence absolute. This is the life of the gods. But other souls, trying to reach the same heights, fail, and fall upon the earth, occupying a higher or lower station as they have more or less truth. But memories of the glories of heaven remain as reminiscence, and the soul by continuous effort and aspiration may again soar upward to regain its lost inheritance."

The allegorical character of this description must not be forgotten. That Plato believed in the pre-existence of the soul, and that its life on earth is a lapse from a perfect condition, is generally assumed, but rests principally on mythical statements. The soul that looks upon true being is the pure thinking activity itself, the divinity within man; the soul that falls to earth takes appearance for reality, opinion for knowledge. Plato affirms that the soul must be freed from the dominion of the senses before it can behold that which truly exists, that to which change and death are foreign. Through its union with a mortal body, it is subject to sensuous needs and greeds, but in its essence it is divine. Accordingly, he distinguishes within it the mortal and irrational from the immortal and rational. The irrational is again divided into two parts; the first, the white horse of the myth, is courage, or will; the second is mere sensuous appetite and desire. Reason, or thought, has its dwelling in the head; courage, in the breast; desire, in the lower regions. Courage is nobler than appetite, but acts frequently without reflection, and belongs to the physiological, natural side of man. A curious theory accounts for the way in which desire is ruled. Reason mirrors pleasant or terrible pictures on the smooth surface of the liver, and by means of imagination alarms or quiets the lower appetites. The liver is the organ of presentiments and of prophetic dreams, which are ascribed to the irrational side of the soul.

Plato constantly teaches that corporeal existence is not true life, and that the soul proclaims its divine origin in its conflict with the body, its love for beauty, its longing for knowledge, its aspiration towards the good. To educate the soul is to bring to consciousness what it is in itself. Plato asserts that what we seem to learn is nothing but reminiscence, that learning is a process of recalling that which we possess already. "The soul, as being immortal, and having been born again many times, and having seen all things that there are, whether in this world or in the world below, has knowledge of them all; and it is no wonder that she should be able to call to remembrance all that she ever knew about virtue and about everything; for as all nature is akin, and the soul has learned all things, there is no difficulty in her eliciting, or as men say, learning all out of a single recollection, if a man is strenuous and does not faint; for all inquiry and all learning is but a recollection."

Hegel thinks that Plato conceives the true nature of consciousness in the doctrine of reminiscence. Spirit includes both subjective and objective, the thinking subject and the object thought. But the two appear sundered at first as the inner and the outer, and must be identified in thought to produce knowledge and science. Images of individual transitory things come from without and are the subject of opinion; but universal thoughts, which alone are true, have their birth in the soul and belong to its essence. We convert what is sensuously perceived into something internal and universal through the act by which we go into ourselves and recall it in the depths of consciousness. There dwells in each man as an immanent faculty of his soul, the organ with which he learns; and the art of instruction is that of turning the soul away from transient sensations and images towards the contemplation of the true and the good. But so far as Plato represents all knowledge as possessed by the individual consciousness in a previous state of existence, it belongs to his figurative way of imagining, by means of the myth, relations of pure thought. The individual consciousness, not as a mere exclusive individual, but as inclusive, universal and divine in its essence, has in itself potentially the content of knowing, which can be developed only through its own activity.

Plato's doctrine of the immortality of the soul is based on its essential nature, which excludes the possibility of its destruction. The soul is the principle of motion, and is inseparably combined with the idea of life. The composite alone is subject to dissolution and decay; but the soul in its essence is simple, self-identical, incapable of any change. Its substance is that which remains ever the same even when involved with external material which seems foreign to itself. I represent by myself one sensuous image after another, but their changes do not affect my thinking activity, which remains in permanent self-identity, recognizing all the images as my production.

Plato's belief in retribution after death is closely connected with his doctrine of immortality. As it is impossible to determine the precise way in which souls are punished, he represented it mythically as transmigration, a theory borrowed from the Pythagoreans. The soul which has yielded to appetite and sensuous desire must enter lower forms of existence; the soul which, through conflict and aspiration, has risen above the corporeal, attains a state of blissful repose. "The process of the world, the history of the universe, has no other import than this perpetual transition of *Psyche* between the higher and the lower, the divine and the human world," says Schwegler. At once spiritual and unspiritual, free and unfree, the two contradictory elements of the soul are manifested as a succession in time. Man is the union of sense and reason; the soul, therefore, is inclined both to the sensuous and the ideal. The solution of this enigma can only be found in its ethical nature and destiny, which is the central point of the Platonic philosophy.

CHAPTER XXII.

THE PLATONIC ETHICS.

TO SOCRATES Plato owed, in part, the purity and fervor of his strivings, his conviction of the necessity of moral knowledge. His lofty idealism lifted ethics to a height, transcended only by Christianity. He sought first to ascertain and establish the ultimate aim of moral activity, or the supreme good; he treated next of its realization in individuals, or virtue; and finally of that toward which all morality tends, the objective actualization of the good in the state.

The good is what all men desire: to possess it is happiness: in what does it consist? Not in this changing and perishable sensuous existence, but in the life of thought, pure contemplation, the endeavor of the soul to become like God. "Evils, Theodorus, can never perish," says Plato, in the Theætetus, "for there must always remain something which is antagonistic to good. Of necessity they hover around this mortal sphere and the earthly nature, having no place among the gods in heaven. Wherefore, also, we ought to fly away thither, and to fly thither is to become like God, as far as this is possible; and to become like Him is to become holy and just and wise."

In other dialogues, the body appears as a fetter, a

dungeon of the soul, the grave of the higher life. The task of the soul is to purify and emancipate itself from corporeal influence, to withdraw from the sensuous into the life of thought. The appetites and passions, the lower element of the soul, seduce us from our true destiny, degrade the human into the animal, and are the root of vice and misery. Philosophy is a means of purification, freeing the soul from its sensuous fetters, and lifting it into the world of Ideas where it beholds the good and the true, regaining the blessedness it had lost through its immersion in matter.

But this withdrawal from finite conditions is a negative theory of morality, which Plato completed by other views, ascribing more importance to the sensible world as that which reveals the Idea. He refutes the doctrine of pleasure as the highest good, because pleasure is relative and is quickly transformed into pain. It is also changing and indefinite, and cannot be the aim of the soul's activity. But a life without pleasure or pain would be pure apathy. The good does not entirely exclude pleasure, but it must be guided by reason so as to produce order and measure. The chief constituent of the Supreme Good is participation in ideal knowledge; the second, the formation of that which is harmonious, beautiful and perfect; the third, mind and wisdom; the fourth, the special sciences, the arts and right opinions; the fifth and last, the pure and painless pleasures of the senses. "We cannot fail to perceive the moderation, the respect for all that is in human nature, the harmonious culture of the whole man, by which the Platonic ethics prove themselves such genuine fruits of the Greek national mind," says Zeller.

The essential means of happiness is virtue, the internal harmony and health of the soul. If passion and appetite rule, the human and divine element in our nature is subjected to the animal; the soul is miserable and enslaved. The virtuous man alone is free and happy; his soul takes hold of the Eternal, for true philosophy and perfect morality are one. Plato transcends the Socratic doctrine of expediency; virtue in itself is its own reward, vice its own punishment. Were it possible for the righteous to be mistaken by God as well as by man, and for the wicked to conceal their wickedness from both, the first would still be happy, the second unhappy. Virtue has unconditional worth, independently of future retribution.

Plato followed Socrates at first, and identified virtue with knowledge, but was led by reflection to modify this view. Although the inclination towards virtue is implanted in human nature itself, he recognized that moral disposition varies according to temperaments and individuals. Ordinary virtue, founded on habit, custom and right opinion, must precede the higher morality, he says in the Republic. The first is presupposed by the second, and the second is perfected by philosophy. He believed, with Socrates, in the unity of virtue, but at the same time admitted a plurality of moral attributes, assigning them to different parts of the soul. The virtue of reason is wisdom, the rule of the soul's life; the virtue of the heart is courage, or valor, which helps reason in the struggle against outward and inward peril; the virtue of sensuous appetite is self-control, or temperance; and finally, the virtue which unites the others that there may be perfect internal harmony, is justice.

Plato attempted no systematic application of his principles to subjective morality. He transcended the ordinary Greek view in his belief that the just man should do good even to his enemies, and ought never to commit suicide, because his life was not his own, but a gift from God.

He was not able to free himself altogether from the defects of Greek morality. He exalted woman mentally and morally, yet misunderstood wholly the ethical import of marriage, regarding it chiefly from a physiological point of view. He shared the contempt of the Greeks for trade and commerce, which relate merely to the satisfaction of bodily wants, and proceed from the lower appetitive part of the soul. He insisted on a just and humane treatment of slaves, but did not object to slavery itself.

"Justice in large letters," morality actualized in the life of the state, objective rather than subjective, is the fundamental principle of Plato's ethics. Eternal right, the Good, is embodied in the constitution of society itself, to which individuals must conform, even at the cost of self-sacrifice, because they have no other way of self-assertion. The idea of political justice is inseparable from that of individual justice, in Plato's thought. The principle of the modern world, subjective freedom, the right of the individual to his own moral conviction, appeared to Plato an element of destruction.

"'The true ideal is not something that merely *ought* to be actual, but that *is* actual,' says Hegel. 'For that which is actual is reasonable. · · · If one would recognize the actuality of substance he must look through the surface on which the passions contend for mastery. The temporal, the perishable, exists, it is true, and it can make needs and wants enough for any one; but nevertheless it is no true actuality, no more than is the particularity of the subject, his wishes and inclinations. If we consider the content of the Platonic Idea, we shall see that Plato has portrayed in the Republic the Greek ethical culture in its most substantial form; the Greek national life is what constitutes the true content of his work. Plato is not the man to busy himself with abstract theories and principles; his true spirit has recognized and unfolded the true; and this could be nothing else than the true in the world in which he lived, this one spirit which was vital in him as well as in Greece. No one can transcend his time; the spirit of his time is also his spirit, but he must see to it that he does not fail to recognize it according to its content."

Justice, according to Plato, is the order of the State, and the State is the outward embodiment of justice under the conditions of human society. The ethical is held fast as the divine substance of the State; the true State should be a pattern of true virtue. It alone can secure the general victory of good over evil. But the only power that can place morality on a firm foundation, free it from contingency, and guarantee its existence and continuance, is philosophy. Proceeding from the State to the individual, from the political and ethical to the moral idea, Plato preserves the true character of Greek thought. What he seeks to discover is the principle which lies at the foundation of society, connecting it with the individual mind, so that the law of the one must be the law of the other.

He divides his citizens into three classes, corresponding to the three parts of the soul. The highest rank is that of the rulers, or learned men, the State guardians; the second is that of the warriors who protect the State and maintain its laws; the third and most numerous is that of the agriculturists and artisans, who provide the necessities of life, laboring for the gratification of sense and appetite.

The only means of advancement is to excel others in knowledge and virtue; exceptional ability of this kind is always rewarded by the State. The ruling class who deliberate concerning the general interest express the idea of wisdom; the warriors, that of courage, fortitude, steadfastness of spirit, the firm assertion of what is just; the laborers, that of temperance or self-control. The qualities of each class interpenetrate the rest, and are brought into harmony though a deeper principle, that of justice, which determines the true relation of all things and persons to each other, and itself a virtue is the universal substance out of which particular virtues arise. To the individual as to the State, justice is so related as to give the supremacy to reason, subjecting the lower part of the soul to the higher, the principle of sense to that of intelligence.

"The just man does not permit the several elements within him to meddle with one another, but he sets in order his own inner life, and is his own master, and at peace with himself; and when he has bound together the three principles within him, which may be compared to the middle, higher, and lower divisions of the scale, and the intermediate intervals, when he has bound together all these, and is no longer many, but has become one entirely temperate and perfectly adjusted nature, then he will begin to act if he has to act, whether in a matter of property, or in the treatment of the body, or some affair of politics or private business; in all which cases he will think and call just and good action that which preserves and coöperates with this condition, and the knowledge which presides over this wisdom; and unjust action that which at any time destroys this, and the opinion which presides over unjust action, ignorance."

The Platonic State is an aristocracy which excludes part of its citizens from any direct share in political power. As in the soul, the smallest part is to rule, so in the State the minority who excel the rest in virtue and intelligence, are alone to govern. Their power is unbounded and unshared. Nothing is more dangerous to a State than to entrust public matters to the incompetent; neither the artisans nor the warriors are to step outside of their respective spheres. The only means of advancement is exceptional ability; the mass of the people are not to meddle either with weapons or with politics. On the other hand, industrial activity is prohibited to the warriors and rulers; they are even forbidden to possess private property, but must devote themselves entirely to the State, and derive their subsistence from the labor of the third class. The State is wise when the rulers are wise; courageous when its warriors are courageous; temperate when the passions of the multitude are restrained by reason and the striving toward the good. When everyone fulfills his appointed duty, and the different classes are united in one organism, justice arises.

The first condition and final aim of the State is the virtue of its citizens. In order to secure this Plato would regulate their whole manner of life and education. He would even place the parentage of the citizens under State control. The children belong to the State alone; they are to be separated from their parents and brought up publicly from the first moment of their existence. The magistrates are to determine their vocation, placing them in the rank for which they seem fitted by natural disposition and character. The higher class are to receive instruction in music, literature, and gymnastics. But Plato admonishes us that even in studying gymnastics we must remember that the soul is related to the body as a cause to an effect, and that the first should be considered rather than the second. Under music, which Plato calls the fortress of the State, he includes poetry and moral culture generally, the development in the soul of that sense of order and harmony which will keep a man steadfast in the right way before he attains scientific knowledge. The mere athlete becomes a savage, the mere musician grows effeminate; the two must be mingled in fair proportions if the soul is to be duly attempered. When a beautiful soul harmonizes with a beautiful form, that will be the fairest of sights to him who has the eye to contemplate the vision.

Art is subordinated to ethics in the Platonic state. The poets, Homer and Hesiod, are banished because their representations of God are unworthy. In so far as their stories of the gods were accepted by the Greeks as universal maxims and divine laws, Plato is justified, although he wholly mistakes the ethical idea which underlies their poetry and constitutes its real substance. True art is not fanciful and imitative, but the expression of the highest moral energy, according to Plato.

After the preparatory discipline in music and gymnastics, the highest class are to receive intellectual training in dialectic, which extends far into manhood. Education should never finish, beginning with gymnastics in youth, and ending with philosophy in maturer life. Then, when nature begins to decay, the soul retires into herself and is the "spectator of all time and all existence."

That the citizens may belong wholly to the state, Plato lays down a rule of life for the two higher classes. They are to have common dwellings and common meals, a community of property, and of wives and children. They can possess neither gold nor silver, but receive a moderate maintenance provided by the third class. Women are to share the education of men in war and in political affairs. Lawyers and physicians will have little to do on account of the virtue of the citizens and their healthy mode of life. If one cannot be cured quickly and simply, it is better to die than to live for the care of a sickly body. The physician shall have personal experience of disease, for he cures with his mind and not with his body. The lawyer, on the other hand, controls mind by mind, and should have no experience of evil. The ideal judge should be advanced in years, should have passed an innocent youth and acquired experience of evil late in life by observation. Virtue can know vice, but vice can never know virtue.

As to the great mass of citizens, the artisans and the agriculturists, they are left to themselves; "for it is not of much importance where the corruption of society and pretension to be what you are not extends only to cobblers; but when the guardians of the laws and of the government are only seemers and not real guardians, that is the utter ruin of the state." Plato probably believed that a certain amount of culture would be diffused from the higher classes to the lower. With his Greek prejudice against industrial activity, he fails to see the economical importance of the laboring classes, just as he ignores their political significance. His government is an aristocracy, but an aristocracy based on the possession of intelligence and virtue.

He foresees the ridicule that will be directed against

his proposition, that the rulers of a state must be philosophers. He explains why it is that the study of philosophy unfits one to be a practical politician. The philosopher is one whose mind is fixed upon the end and meaning of things, their substance and reality. The rest of the world are following images and shadows, blindly feeling after the good. The philosopher must either descend to this pursuit, where he necessarily stumbles and deserves contempt, or he must keep his own high course, which as unintelligible is despised. But how would it be if when he has come out into the light where he sees all things as they are, he neither glorifies himself by living apart from men, nor confuses his light with their darkness, but dwelling in the midst of them seeks rather to lead them upward by the same path which he has followed? Philosophy, then, would harmonize with politics; the moving spring of the state would not be the self-seeking principle, but the divine Idea leading men towards the good.

The most striking peculiarity of the Platonic republic is the entire subordination of the individual to the state, the exclusion of subjective freedom. That individual inclination should be ignored in the choice of a vocation, is opposed to modern thought. It is not for one man to prescribe for another that he shall follow this or that vocation, that he shall become a shoemaker, or a lawyer, or a soldier. It is his right as a person to decide the matter for himself without regard to external circumstances.

To do away with the principle of private property is another violation of subjective freedom. Property is a possession which belongs to me as this particular person, and through it I exist as an abstract individual self. The laborers, tradesmen and agriculturists of the Platonic state produce the necessaries of life for all, and the producer like the rest uses from the common store whatever he needs. The objection brought by Aristotle against this view is still valid, that it would take from men the stimulus to activity. Property, according to Hegel, is an object into which I have introduced my will, and by this act I have made it mine, so that he who touches it touches me, and touches that will which is the substance of my personality. "The essential point is that my free-will takes the first necessary step toward becoming objectively real in the possession of actual objects," says Professor Morris, in his interpretation of Hegel's thought, "and the essential truth is that just as the free-will cannot be conceived as a mere means to an end foreign to itself, so property, being according to its true conception and definition only the primary form in which the free-will renders itself objectively real, has something of the like character of an absolute end, and is proportionately sacred and inviolable."

The doctrine in Plato that has excited most horror is not a community of property, but a community of wives and children. How could this great moral teacher have so misunderstood and violated the sanctity of the family? There is no sentiment or imagination in his conception of marriage; his one aim is to improve the race without regard to individual inclination. The Greek exalted friendship above love, and looked upon the family as a customary institution, necessary but not sacred like the state. Professor Jowett reminds us that the side from which Plato regarded the social problem is one from which we habitually turn away. "That the most important influence on human life should be wholly left to chance or shrouded in mystery, and instead of being disciplined or understood, should be required to conform only to an external standard of propriety, cannot be regarded by the philosopher as a safe or satisfactory condition of human things."

Plato felt the necessity of a universal community in the life of man, the truth implied in the existence of society and realized historically in the doctrines of Christianity. The ends for which he strove were high and noble, but he fell into grave errors as to the means that should be used for their attainment. The self-will of individuals had been the ruin of Athens and of Greece, and in excluding it from his Republic, he did not see that he was converting the individual into a mere instrument of the state, and that the subjective side is as essential to the realization of freedom as the objective. This is the limit of Plato's thought of the state, and it was the limit of his age. "The deficiency of subjectivity is the deficiency of the Greek ethical idea itself." (Hegel.)

Plato sought to stifle the passions and inclinations of men and exclude selfishness, by excluding property and family life and the choice of occupation; all of which relate to the principle of subjective freedom. He clearly recognized that when individuals pursue private aims and interests without regard to the common welfare, the destruction of the state is imminent

But the soul of man is in itself an absolute end and aim, and justice demands that each individual, by his own self-conscious knowing and willing, shall enter into harmony with other individuals through institutions, the family, society and the state.

Plato condemned the particular interest of the individual as an unworthy factor in the ethical organism of the State. But this is abstract rather than concrete freedom. The opposite of his principle, the setting up of the private will of the individual as a supreme authority, has been advocated in modern times by Rousseau and others. But this view is equally one-sided and abstract.

The State must not ignore the particular opinions and volitions of individuals, but must realize through them the universal will and interest of man. The individual, on the other hand, must not devote himself exclusively to that which is private and special, but must comprehend the public interest as his interest, obeying the law not as an external but an internal command. To constitute true freedom the particular interests of the individual must harmonize with the universal aims of man. Either alone, abstracted from the other, is but one side of the truth.

ÆSTHETIC.

A famous side of the Platonic philosophy is the Æsthetic, the science of the Beautiful. The two elements which constitute the beautiful are the sensuous phenomenon and the idea; that which is beautiful in the sensuous is spiritual, the idea shining through it visibly. Fairer than the beautiful body is the beautiful soul; fairest of all is the pure Idea of the Beautiful to which nothing material clings. All that is good is beautiful; Truth, Beauty and Goodness, three in one, constitute the Platonic Trinity.

CONCLUSION.

"This may be given as the chief content of the Platonic Philosophy," says Hegel; "first, the accidental form of discourse in which noble free men converse without other interests than that of the spiritual life of Theory; secondly, they come, led only by the content, to the deepest ideas and most beautiful thoughts like precious stones which one finds, if not exactly in a desert, yet upon a dry journey; thirdly, there is found no systematic connection, though all flows from one common interest; fourthly, the subjectivity of the Idea is everywhere lacking; but, fifthly, the substantial Idea forms the basis."

THE OLDER ACADEMY.

Plato's instructions had assembled in the Academy a numerous circle of hearers, many of whom attracted by his fame came from distant countries. It is due to him more than to any other individual that Athens retained her intellectual supremacy even after her loss of political power.

Plato's immediate successor was his nephew Speusippus, followed after eight years by Xenocrates, and later by other disciples. These various teachers professed to maintain Plato's doctrine unaltered, but seem to have neglected dialectic and the theory of Ideas, and to have inclined more and more to Pythagoreanism and religious mysticism. But we know so little of their teachings that we cannot speak of them authoritatively. "Only a portion of Plato's spiritual legacy descended with his garden to the Academy," says Zeller; "the full inheritance passed over to Aristotle, who was thereby qualified to transcend his master."

CHAPTER XXIII.

LIFE AND WRITINGS OF ARISTOTLE.

"ARISTOTLE is one of the deepest and richest scientific geniuses that ever lived," says Hegel, "a man without equal in ancient and modern times. To characterize in brief his labors one would say that he has traveled over the whole range of human knowledge, has pushed his investigations on all sides into the real universe, and has brought into subjection to Ideas the wealth and untamed luxuriance of the realms of nature."

He was born in the year 384 B. C., at Stagira, a city in Thrace, colonized by Greeks. To his birthplace he owes the famous appellation of "The Stagirite," given to him in later days. His father, Nicomachus, was the physician and friend of the Macedonian King Amyutas. All his ancestors were physicians, tracing their pedigree to the son of Esculapius. We have no means of knowing how far this inheritance influenced his scientific activity, much of the testimony concerning his early life being untrustworthy.

He came to Athens in his seventeenth year, and entered the school of Plato, where he remained for twenty years until his master's death. We cannot doubt that during this time he laid the foundation of that wonderful knowledge and erudition which enabled him afterward to comprehend in his system of thought all earlier speculations, enriched by multifarious allusions that prove he was as keen a student of nature as of men and books. It is said that Plato called Aristotle the "mind of the school." Aristotle regarded Plato as a revered and honored teacher, notwithstanding his apparent unfairness in the criticism of Plato's philosophy. "The bad may not even praise Plato," he says.

It is not known why Speusippus rather than Aristotle was chosen as Plato's successor in the Academy. On account of this slight, or for other reasons, Aristotle left Athens immediately after the death of Plato to reside at the court of Hermias, prince of Atarneus, in Mysia. He was accompanied by Plato's faithful disciple Xenocrates, a proof of the friendly relations subsisting between Aristotle and his master. Hermias was afterward betrayed into the hands of the Persians and crucified, and Aristotle fled to Mitylene with his wife.

From Mitylene Aristotle was called by Philip, King of Macedon, to superintend the education of his son Alexander, then thirteen years old. "The culture of Alexander is a sufficient reply to all the prating about the practical usefulness of speculative philosophy," says Hegel. Aristotle sought to develop and strengthen the inborn greatness of Alexander's mind and character, to lead him to perfect self-possession and independence. It is in part owing to his wise teacher that Alexander was a thinker and a student as well as a world-conqueror, and that, even amid his later excesses and temptations, he never ceased to reverence moral truth and beauty. He was enabled through his conquests to scatter far and wide the germs of Greek culture, with the conscious purpose of elevating those whom he subjugated. He never forgot the interests of art and science, sending to Aristotle either specimens, or drawings, or descriptions, of whatever new animals and plants he found in Asia. He always regarded Aristotle with love and respect, although a certain coldness sprang up between the two in later years.

After Alexander's departure for Asia, Aristotle returned to Athens, and opened a school of philosophy in a gymnasium called the Lyceum. His school derived the name Peripatetic from the avenues of shade trees where the great teacher walked, as he conversed on philosophy with a few favorite disciples. He is said to have delivered acroamatic (or technical) and exoteric discourses, the first on abstract metaphysical doctrines to a chosen circle of hearers, the second on educational topics to the general public. But it is clear that the discourses of a philosopher, whether technical or popular, are the product of his thought, which alone gives significance to his utterances. "One may see for himself which works of Aristotle are really speculative and philosophic," says Hegel, "and which ones are to a greater extent of a merely empirical nature; they are not for this reason, however, to be looked upon as opposite in content as though Aristotle wrote some things for the people and other things for his intimate disciples."

The work that he accomplished during the twelve years that he taught in Athens appears incredible. All his writings belong to this period. The stupendous task which he achieved was nothing less than to found and elaborate the deepest and most comprehensive system of philosophy that the world has ever known.

On the death of Alexander, a sudden storm of opposition against his successor broke out in Athens. Aristotle was regarded as a member of the Macedonian party, and from political reasons was accused of impiety. He fled to Chalcis in Euboea, that "the Athenians might not have a second opportunity to sin against philosophy." He died there in his sixty-third year, following in death one great contemporary, Alexander, and preceding another, Demosthenes.

The moral personality of Aristotle as it is revealed in his writings, in his last will and testament, and in the few facts that we possess concerning his life, is high and pure. He was grateful to his benefactors, gentle and humane in his treatment of slaves and dependents, a loyal friend, and a loving husband. In his noble conception of marriage he went far beyond the views of his countrymen. His morality was supported by a comprehensive knowledge of humanity and the deepest reflection; it had nothing in it one-sided and exaggerated.

Never has the world seen such great and different gifts united in one person as in Aristotle. He was both a scientist and a speculative philosopher, a close observer of the empirical facts of nature and an interpreter of their hidden significance, analyzing rigidly individual differences and particularities without losing sight of their relation and unity.

His style of exposition is less artistic but more

scientific than that of Plato. Exactness and definiteness are his aim rather than beauty; he limits himself strictly to the problem of knowledge. He lacks the Platonic fervor and enthusiasm, but surpasses his master in the ripeness of his judgment and his many-sided and thorough investigation of every domain of knowledge.

Whatever may have been his means of help, we must regard with awe the achievements of Aristotle, executed in one brief human life, the conquest of a strong soul over a weakly body. He designated to philosophy its course for centuries, and mapped out for the Greeks the points they had reached in scientific culture, illuminated by his own original thought and inquiries. Seldom has one so truly fulfilled his historical mission, so gloriously solved the scientific problems bequeathed to him by his predecessors; and we cannot but believe from the evidence of his work that the man was as great and admirable as the philosopher.

Aristotle left behind him a great many manuscripts, but it is uncertain whether we possess a single one in a genuine and uninjured shape. A strange story is told of their fate for two centuries. Aristotle, it is said, bequeathed his library, including these manuscripts, to Theophrastus. It was the first important library in Greece, collected by means of Aristotle's wealth and the assistance of Alexander. Theophrastus, in his turn, bequeathed it to his pupil Neleus, and the heirs of Neleus, fearing that the king of Pergamus would seize Aristotle's writings for his own royal library, concealed them in a cellar, where they were forgotten and badly injured. A century later, they were discovered and sold to Appelicon of Teos, who filled up the gaps to the best of his ability and gave them to the public. Soon after Appelicon's death the Roman Sulla conquered Athens, and the writings of Aristotle were among his spoils. From Sulla they passed into the possession of a Greek grammarian, Tyrannion; from Tyrannion copies were received by Andronicus of Rhodes, the Peripatetic, who made a catalogue of their contents, and sent them forth in a new and improved edition.

The story assumes that the writings of Aristotle were inaccessible to students for nearly two centuries, and is refuted by Zeller and other authorities, who find in the works of these same centuries traces of an acquaintance with their principal doctrines.

What cannot be denied is the fact that many of Aristotle's manuscripts are badly disfigured, that they are incomplete and full of omissions, that individual parts are disconnected, that verbal repetitions occur, all going to prove the injury they have suffered. Zeller thinks this is due in part to the circumstances under which they were composed and published, to the use that was made of them in instruction, and to the ignorance of editors and copyists. Fortunately we have enough that is genuine to enable us to form a definite idea of the Aristotelian philosophy, not only in its extent and compass, but in many of its details.

The writings of Aristotle passed from the Greeks

into the hands of Arabian scholars and commentators. They became known to the western world in the twelfth and thirteenth centuries, and formed the basis of Scholasticism. "To the ancients, Aristotle was 'Nature's Private Secretary;' to the middle ages, after 1150, he was simply 'The Philosopher,' or 'The Master of those that know;' and, though, for a brief period, his sun was eclipsed by reactionary influences, philosophers of nearly all modern schools, as well as scientists and poets, have vied with each other in doing him honor. Among these may be mentioned Leibnitz, Lessing, Goethe, Hegel, Cuvier, Bain."

In point of subject-matter, the writings of Aristotle may be divided into physical, metaphysical, logical and ethical. This classification is made for convenience, and was not adopted by Aristotle himself, who nowhere supplies any scheme or skeleton or general division of his system of philosophy.

CHAPTER XXIV.

GENERAL CHARACTER OF THE ARISTOTELIAN PHILOSOPHY.

"THE subject-matter of philosophy is the most knowable," says Aristotle; "to-wit, principles and causes. For through these, and by these, all other things are known; principles are, however, not to be known through substitutes." Aristotle here takes his stand against the ordinary mode of view; the knowledge he seeks to gain is the knowledge of final causes. "Man has come to philosophy through wonder," he says. "Wherefore if men began to philosophize in order to escape ignorance, it is clear that they pursued scientific knowledge for the sake of knowing it, and not for any utility it might possess. This is also shown by the entire external course of events. For first after men have supplied their necessary wants and those requisite for ease and comfort, they have begun to seek philosophical knowledge. Therefore they seek it for no ulterior utility; and as we say that a free man is one who exists only for his own sake, and not for the sake of another, thus is philosophy the free science among sciences, for it alone exists for itself—a knowing of knowing. * * * Other sciences may be more necessary than philosophy, but none is more excellent."

This doctrine is like that of Socrates and Plato. But Aristotle differs from his master in connecting philosophy more closely with experience. Plato denies any real worth to the world of the changing and becoming except so far as its contradictions lead us away from it to the contemplation of pure Ideas; eternity, the supra-sensible world, are more real to him than the affairs of this life. Aristotle, on the other hand, finds a more positive relation between thought and experience, not holding them apart abstractly, but comprehending both in concrete unity. Plato cared little for the individual appearance, the variety and multiplicity of things, seeking only to know concepts, Ideas. Aristotle agrees with Plato that knowledge has to do with the universal essence of things, but he regards it as his especial problem to derive the individual from the universal, to explain appearances. He declares that science relates to the customary, what usually happens, as well as to the necessary, and must seek to reach approximate truth, the greatest possible probability, where absolute certainty is unattainable. "Why should he who thirsts after knowledge," he says, "refuse to seek some where he cannot have all?"

To identify Aristotle's method with empiricism is incorrect, although his procedure might warrant such an assumption. "But he is in the deepest sense speculative," says Hegel. "All sides of knowing enter his mind, all interest him; all are handled by him with depth and exhaustiveness. Abstraction may easily get confused in the empirical extent of a phenomenon, and be at a loss how to find its application and verification, and be obliged at last to take up with a partial procedure without being able to exhaust all the phases of the phenomenon. Aristotle, however, in that he takes into consideration all sides of the universe, seizes the whole of each individual sphere, as a speculative philosopher, and treats it in such a manner as to arrive at its deepest speculative idea."

His method, like that of Socrates and Plato, is dialectic, but he unites with it the observation of a natural scientist. He examines the thoughts of the earlier philosophers, corrects their one-sidedness, investigates the subject from contradictory points of view, and finally passes to the speculative consideration of the whole matter. He thus seems to be empirical while he is really philosophical; "for the empirical, comprehended in its synthesis, is the speculative idea."

"Aristotle moves essentially on the ground and in the direction of the Socratic-Platonic dialectic," says Zeller; "he developed the Socratic induction to conscious technique, completed it by the doctrine of demonstration, whose especial creator he is, and by all the discussion therewith connected, and gave in his writings the most perfect model of a dialectic investigation, strictly and sharply carried through from one side to all sides. If we did not know it otherwise, we should recognize in his scientific procedure the pupil of Plato."

Aristotle unites with dialectic a close and rigid scrutiny of the facts of the physical world. The philosopher, according to his thought, must not lose sight of the efficient and material causes of things while seeking their concept and final end. Aristotle is not merely one of the most speculative thinkers, but a careful and unwearied observer, a diligent and erudite scholar. Experience is for him material to be developed into thought. He supports his philosophic structure upon a basis of physical knowledge, attained through a many-sided examination and study of facts and appearances. We shall not find in him the exactness of procedure demanded by empirical science in modern times; the world was yet too young, means of help were wanting to exact observation, the science of mathematics was not far enough advanced. Aristotle's work in this field was that of a pioneer; he could not be expected to discriminate as carefully as later investigators between the empirical and the philosophical methods of inquiry.

His style is severely logical, and therefore lacks the dramatic and artistic perfection of the Platonic dialogue. He verifies every step of his process with rigid exactness, and clothes his thought in dry technical prose rather than in poetic myth or graceful conversation. His speech is purely scientific, and in this respect surpasses that of his master.

If we take a general view of his system of thought we shall find it resting upon a Socratic-Platonic basis, yet at the same time original and independent, offering an entirely new solution of the way in which thought is related to matter. Essential being, according to Plato, is only to be found in the world of eternal ideas, apart from appearances; but, for Aristotle, the idea as the essence of things cannot be separated from things themselves, it is the form toward which the sensuous strives with inner necessity. It is one and the same being that exists undeveloped as potentiality, developed as actuality. The world of the changing and becoming is thus explained, and at the heart of things we find infinite energy.

There is no systematic classification and division of Aristotle's philosophy. He goes from particular to particular and seems always to be philosophizing on the individual, the special. "He obtains thus a plurality of coördinated sciences," says Schwegler, "each one of which has its independent foundation, but no highest science which should comprehend all."

According to the later Peripatetics, Aristotle divides philosophy into theoretical and practical, the one treating of knowledge whose end is found in itself, the other of knowledge relating to action and conduct. Theoretical philosophy is again subdivided into mathematics, physics, and "first philosophy." He also speaks of a third form of knowledge, relating to the artistic creation of works of art. But this classification is not adopted by Aristotle himself, nor does he furnish us anywhere a general outline or summary of his system.

CHAPTER XXV.

ARISTOTLE'S LOGIC.

ARISTOTLE is the father of logic, as Euclid is the father of geometry. He has discovered and described the formal activity of the pure understanding for all time. His writings on this subject are comprised under the name Organon. Aristotle himself did not use the word Logic, which was probably invented afterwards by the Stoics; he spoke of Analytic, by which he meant the science of analyzing the forms of reasoning. "There is the same course to be pursued in philosophy, and in every science or branch of knowledge," he says. "You must study facts. Experience alone can give general principles on any subject. . . . . When the facts in each branch are brought together, it will be the province of the logician to set out the demonstrations in a manner clear and fit for use. When the investigation into nature is complete, you will be able in some cases to exhibit a demonstration; in other cases you will have to say that demonstration is not attainable."

Aristotle treats first of the universal predicates of being, the Categories. The object of our thinking must fall under the following heads: Substance, quantity, quality, relation, where, when, position, possession, action, passion. These categories present the different sides from which things can be regarded, but do not describe their real nature.

The most important category is substance, which in a strict sense is the individual. It is the original unchangeable essence in each thing, different from everything derived. All the other categories lead back to substance, and express either its attributes or determinations. The treatment of this question is therefore ontological, and belongs to metaphysics as well as to logic.

Knowledge relates to the essence of things, the universal, to final causes. But the universal can only be known through the individual; causes can only be known through effects. The soul carries in itself the ground of its knowing, but this knowing is developed only through experience. What in itself is first is for us last. The first for us is sensuous perception, which sees the individual; but in the individual the universal is implicit. We are thus led from the appearance to the essence, from effects to causes.

The concept is an expression of the essence of that which it denotes. But essence relates only to form; we can have no concept of the sensuous in itself. We can define, not this sensuous object, but this definite manner of sensuous existence, the general form of the object. Every concept includes, or may include, many single things; thought and its interpreter, language, seek ever the universal.

The concept forms the starting point for all scientific investigation, and is at the same time the aim toward which it strives. Knowing is nothing more than insight into the ground of things, and this insight is completed in the concept; the *what* is the same as the *why*, we cognize the concept of a thing when we cognize its cause.

The concept in itself is neither true nor false; something must be affirmed or denied of it in order to constitute a proposition. To the concept, or the noun, a verb must be added. When this is done we have a judgment, which is necessarily true or false. Every affirmation is opposed to a denial, so that either the one or the other must be true, and no third is possible. Hence the principle of contradiction and of excluded third or middle. "Of the affirmation and the negation of the same thing, the one is always false, the other true." Between the two terms of a contradiction there is no mean; it is necessary either to affirm or to deny every predicate of every subject."

"Aristotle was the first to name the syllogism," says Zeller, "and to observe that every connection and advance of our thinking rests on the syllogistic joining of judgments. The word, indeed, existed before, but Aristotle stamped it with the technical meaning which it has ever since borne. "In introducing the word, it must not be supposed that he introduced, or invented, the process of reasoning to which he applied it, or that he even pretended to do so," says Sir Alexander Grant. "The grammarian who first distinguished nouns from verbs and gave them their names, did not invent nouns and verbs, but only called attention to their existence in language; and he who first made rules of syntax was only recording the ways in which men naturally speak and write, not making innovations in language; and so Aristotle with his syllogism only clearly pointed out a process which had always, though unconsciously, been carried on. There is no doubt that, ever since they have possessed reason at all, men have made syllogisms, though like M. Jourdain speaking prose, they have for the most part been unconscious of it."

Aristotle defines the syllogism as a form of ratiocination in which, from certain premises and through their means, something farther and different from them necessarily follows. Every syllogism must contain three concepts, and only three, one of which, the middle term, is either subject in one of the premises and predicate in the other (first figure), or predicate in both premises (second figure), or subject in both (third figure).

Upon the basis of the syllogism is built the theory of scientific demonstration, which Aristotle established in the second Analytic. Knowing consists in the knowledge of causes, and the cause of an appearance is that from which it necessarily proceeds. Proof is a conclusion from necessary premises, but may include in a conditioned way that which occurs usually. The purely accidental can neither be proved nor known. But the necessary is only that which belongs to the essence and the concept of the object; therefore the concept of everything is that from which demonstration proceeds and toward which it strives. "Its problem consists in this," says Zeller, " it must not only show the determinations that belong to every object by virtue of its concept, but also the mediations through which they are brought to it; it must derive the particular from the universal, appearances from their causes."

Aristotle maintains that there is a necessary limit to this mediatory knowing. Whether we ascend from the particular to the universal, from the subject which is not a predicate to ever higher predicates, or descend from the most universal, the predicate which is not a subject, to the particular, we reach a point where further progress is impossible; otherwise, there could be neither demonstration nor concept. To prove everything is impossible: "Science must commence with something which is not proved at all," says Aristotle. It must start from immediate principles which cannot be established by any syllogistic reasoning. The axioms of Euclid are a specimen of such principles. But every science has its own; its first truths must consist of indemonstrable definitions. Their certainty is recognized by an immediate activity of the reason, an activity that is only gradually developed by experience, according to Aristotle.

All scientific knowing proceeds either deductively from the universal to the individual or inductively from the individual to the universal. "The prior and more cognizable for us," is what lies nearest to the sphere of sensation, but "the absolutely prior and more cognizable" is what is most remote from that sphere. That which is clear in itself is the intelligible; that which is more evident to us is the sensible. The limits of knowledge are, on the one hand, the individual; on the other, the most general. It is more scientific to pass from the "prior in nature" to the "prior for us," from the condition to the conditioned; but for those who cannot follow this order the inverse one must be employed. "Plunged in the world of the senses, we must learn by degrees to discern the object of reason."

Induction is necessarily imperfect because it is impossible to know all individuals. This lack of knowledge Aristotle seeks to supply by proofs of probability. He finds in dialectic a means of help so far as it considers the different sides from which an object may be regarded. It is not strange that his procedure is open to criticism from the standpoint of the modern scientist when we consider the means at our disposal for empirical investigation. To appreciate his real service in the observation and collection of facts, and his acuteness in their explanation, we must judge him by the knowledge and scientific instruments of help possessed by his age.

"To have reorganized and defined the forms that thinking takes in us, is the immortal achievement of Aristotle," says Hegel. "For what interests us otherwise is the concrete thinking absorbed in outer intuition; those forms constitute a net of infinite movableness sunk therein, and to fix these fine threads drawing through everything is a masterpiece of empiricism, and this consciousness is of absolute worth."

The mental activity that Aristotle explains logically is the activity of the understanding. It therefore appears as if thinking were something subjective, and its laws merely formal, without content. The thing in itself may be something quite different from the object of our thought. It is what Hegel calls the logic of the finite, and must add to itself the logic of the infinite in order to attain truth. The forms of thought must be regarded in their totality, which is at the same time subjective and objective. Their content is then the speculative idea, and the logic of understanding becomes the logic of reason.

CHAPTER XXVI.

ARISTOTLE'S METAPHYSICS.

IN the "First Philosophy," or the "Metaphysics," as it is termed to-day, the speculative idea of Aristotle is unfolded. The work is not a connected whole, but several sketches which follow one main idea, not always clearly written or well arranged.

Aristotle defines pure philosophy as "the science of what exists, in so far as it exists, and what pertains to it in-and-for-itself." In the sphere of scientific knowledge that is the highest which relates to the ultimate causes of things, and is therefore First Philosophy, or wisdom. The word Metaphysics—things that follow after physics—was first used by Aristotle's scholars.

Every science supposes three distinct elements, the subject which is demonstrated, the attribute which demonstrates, and the axiom, the principle of demonstration. It shows the relation of a subject to an attribute in a thesis of which it is the only judge. Metaphysics co-ordinates all these theses by superior axioms; it is the universal science. The categories are its genera; Being-in-itself is the common basis of categories and propositions. Being is that of which everything is affirmed and which affirms nothing.

Aristotle begins with a sketch of the history of philosophy. This is necessary in order to explain its terms, the result of the theories of former ages. He carefully examines the views of his predecessors, who began by inquiring after the material principle, then advanced gradually to the idea of motive power or efficient cause, but never clearly developed form or essence and the final cause. He censures the old Ionians for having made a single element the primitive substance, when the sensuous changes of bodies are conditioned by the opposition of elements. Heraclitus committed the same mistake in representing his first principle as fire, and in his more important affirmation of the Becoming, "the flow of all things", he overlooked the fact that change itself presupposes a substratum which is unchanged and unchangeable.

Empedocles first introduced the principle of motion, but did not make clear the difference between his two efficient causes, love and hate, since love not only unites but also separates, and hate not only separates but also unites. To the views of Empedocles concerning substance, Aristotle objects that they would make qualitative change impossible. Against the Atomists he proves that atoms which are only quantitatively different and do not influence each other cannot explain the reciprocal action of bodies, becoming and change. The physics of Anaxagoras is related to that of Empedocles and the Atomists; but Aristotle acknowledges the great service of this philospher in positing *nous*, or intelligence, as the principle of all things.

As to the Eleatics Aristotle asserts that their theories contain no principle for the explanation of appearances. They deny becoming and the multiplicity of things, overlooking the fact that while nothing becomes from absolute non-being, everything becomes from relative non-being. Zeno's arguments against motion are equally one-sided with those of Parmenides against non-being, change and becoming; space and time are treated as discrete quantities, and not as continuous, whereas they are both. The principle of Pythagoras, number, is also defective in not explaining motion and change, the basis of all natural occurrences.

Aristotle's view of the Sophists is already known; their wisdom was but apparent, and concerned only the transient and unreal. He acknowledged the greatness of Socrates, but sought to prove that his work as a philosopher was limited to ethical inquiries, and did not include the setting-up of a metaphysical principle.

It is in Aristotle's criticism of the Platonic Ideas that we discover the essential difference between his system of thought and that of Plato. Aristotle agrees with Plato that only the universal essence of things can be known, that it is necessary to go beyond the transient appearance to its underlying reality. But he denies that the universal is something substantial for itself outside of appearances, for how can an essence and that of which it is the essence exist apart? He says that Plato's ideas are only "things of sense immortalized and eternized," incapable of explaining the world of appearances, and furthermore making it impossible. What is the imperishable substance in the idea man outside of the individuals who participate in this idea? How are we to conceive this participation in the idea if the individual is wholly sundered from the universal? In every case, says Aristotle, we shall have to assume a third man, a prototype of the supersensuous idea of man, and of its sensuous manifestation, individual man. In assuming a double series of sensuous and non-sensuous substances under one and the same name, the adherents of the ideal theory resemble men who increase their numbers in order to facilitate the process of counting. Aristotle criticises especially the immobility of the idea, its entire lack of causality to produce change or to explain nature. We recognize the spirit of the natural scientist who seeks to determine actuality through a full and complete elucidation of facts.

With Aristotle as with Plato the idea is related to an objective reality; but the one teaches its transcendent existence, the other its immanence in the the sensuous appearance, the noumenon in the phenomenon. Socrates, through his investigation of the nature of concepts, led the way to the theory of Ideas; but Socrates never separated the universal from the individuals included under it, or set it outside of the world of real things. Aristotle represents clearly the weakness of the Platonic theory, though some of his objections rest on misinterpretations. He unites the realism of the natural scientist with Plato's logical idealism, and the more he finds to disapprove in his predecessors the more he seeks to answer their unsolved problems.

Hegel explains clearly and decisively the nature of

the antithesis between the Ideas of Plato and Aristotle. The Idea in Plato is in itself essentially concrete and determined; its defect, or one-sidedness, is that it is only in-itself, or potential; it is inert, and does not yet express the activity of the process of actualization. The Idea in Plato is the objective, the good, the final cause, the universal in general; it lacks the principle of vital subjectivity as the moment of actuality, although this principle is implicitly contained in his definition of the Absolute as the unity of opposites. But Aristotle defines it more precisely as Energy, whose nature it is to dirempt, or duplicate this being-for-itself; for, as Aristotle says, "The Entelechy sunders."

The affirmative principle, mere abstract self-identity, is the highest with Plato; Aristotle develops the principle of negativity, or individualization, as distinction or difference, not in the sense of a contingent and merely special subjectivity, but of the pure subjectivity. Aristotle asserts that being and non-being are not the same, but he does not mean by this pure being or non-being, the abstraction which is but the transition of the one into the other; he understands under that *which is* substance, idea, Reason, in the sense of an active final cause. On the one hand he sets up the Universal against the principle of mere change; on the other he defends the principle of activity against the Pythagorean system of numbers and the Platonic system of ideas. "Aristotle's category of activity is change, but a change posited within the Universal, change remaining self-identical; consequently a determining which is self-determining, and therefore the self-realizing, universal *final cause;* in mere change, on the contrary, self-preservation is not necessarily involved. This is the chief doctrine added to philosophy by Aristotle."

Aristotle defines and investigates four metaphysical principles: First, Form or Essence; secondly, Matter or substance; thirdly, the principle of Motion, or Efficient Cause; and fourthly, the Final Cause, or the Good. Closely examined, the four resolve themselves into the single antithesis of matter and form. Thus, in a house, the building materials are the matter, its architectural idea the form, the efficient cause the builder, the completed structure the end or final cause. The efficient cause, the builder, converts the matter (potentiality) into form (actuality). The efficient cause is therefore identical with the formal; the form of the statue in the mind of the sculptor is the cause of the motion through which it is produced. Form and end also coincide, as both are united in the actual statue.

In the relation of form to matter Aristotle discovers the possibility of the becoming. His predecessors argued that what becomes can neither originate from what is nor from what is not; Aristotle seeks to prove that what becomes is and is not relatively at the same time. The uneducated man who becomes educated must contain in himself the ability for culture; all becoming is a transition of potentiality into reality. That which becomes warm must have been formerly cold, that which becomes knowledge must have been formerly ignorance; but cold in itself cannot be transformed into warmth, nor ignorance into knowledge; the becoming is a transition from one condition into the opposite condition.

The presupposition of the becoming, the substrate of change, Aristotle calls matter. It is that which remains when we abstract from all which is the result of becoming, substance without determination or distinction, that which is everything potentially and nothing really, pure potentiality. It is as little non-being as being, it is rather possible being. In itself it is unknowable because it is without determination; we can only attain to its concept through analogy. Conceived as a counterpart to form it is a positive negative.

The concepts of the real and the potential are applied by Aristotle in the same way as those of form and matter. One and the same thing may be related to another as matter and form, in that the potential, in this the real; wood to the finished house is matter, to the growing tree form.

In the development of potentiality (matter) to actuality (form), different degrees are to be distinguished. The lowest degree is matter, absolutely formless, pure potentiality; the highest is form without matter, pure actuality, absolute Spirit. Between the two extremes is a gradation of existences which are both matter and form, the first continually translating itself into the second.

Matter, as the formless and indefinite, is that from which chance in nature proceeds. Aristotle understands by the accidental that which may or may not happen to a thing, which is not contained in its essence and does not therefore occur necessarily. He finds the ground of the accidental in the nature of the finite, or of matter, which as the indefinite contains the possibility of opposite determinations. The accidental happens through the influence of external circumstances. A man digs a hole in the ground for the purpose of finding water, and discovers a hidden treasure; the final aim of the digging is disturbed by a mediate cause.

But Aristotle finds something more positive than the accidental in the nature of matter or substance; he regards it as the seat of motion or change, of a striving after form, and finally as the ground of individual existence. It is difficult to comprehend what he means by this since he regards the individual alone as something substantial, and yet places the ground of actuality in form. On the one side, he recognizes with Plato that the object of knowledge is the concept, the universal; on the other, he asserts that the universal does not lie outside of the individual. He does not explain how the two are related as form and matter, or how the individual that is both form and substance should appear real if the ground of reality lies in form alone.

He has been interpreted differently by different commentators, but the explanation of Hegel is the clearest. Hegel finds in the Aristotelian substance three movements, the first of which has a matter differing from its actual form, and is consequently finite. The second contains the activity which is the object of its process. "This is the in-and-for-itself determined understanding whose content is the final cause which it actualizes through its activity without undergoing change like the mere sensuous substance. For the soul is essentially entelechy, a general process of determination which posits itself; not a merely formal activity whose content comes from elsewhere." The third and highest substance is that in which potentiality, activity, and entelechy are united,—the Absolute Substance.

Through his distinction of form and matter, of the real and the potential, Aristotle was able to solve many of the difficulties of earlier philosophers. He could explain how one can be at the same time many, how soul and body are one being, how finally becoming and change are possible. If matter and form are related as the potential to the actual it lies in the concept of the first to become the second, and the second is the reality of the first. Matter moves towards form and develops itself to reality; form on the other hand makes the potential real, and is the energy of matter.

But the energy of matter is motion, the transition from the possible to the real. "Motion is the perfection of matter through the determination of form, for matter as such is mere potentiality which has in no respect attained reality." Nothing comes from that which is neither potential nor active. Motion is a mediator between potential and actual being, a possibility that strives toward reality, a reality bound in possibility and therefore incomplete. The merely potential cannot produce motion, for it lacks energy: the actual cannot produce motion, for there is nothing in it imperfect and undeveloped; motion can only be comprehended as the working of the actual, or form, upon the potential, or matter.

Motion, with Aristotle, is as eternal as form and matter, whose essential relation it represents. It presupposes a moving cause, itself unmoved, Absolute Spirit,—God. Without this first cause motion would be impossible, since that which exists potentially may or may not become actual and could not be a principle of movement. Aristotle defines the Absolute Essence as pure activity, the *actus purus* of scholastic philosophy. "God is the substance that contains within His potentiality also his actuality inseparably united."—(Hegel).

The actual in the highest sense can only be pure form without substance, the moving force and aim of the world. There is that which is moved and does not move, matter; that which is at once mover and moved, nature; and God, the unmoved mover. The universe forms a continuous system of ascending progression from the first formless substance to its final end and aim—Absolute Goodness and Perfection, or Deity.

Nature is permeated by the substantial thought which gives it life and moves it with constant unrest and desire; it works unconsciously for the sole and single aim of divine reason. It is disposed in an ascending series of terms more and more individualized, each of which includes the preceding and points to a superior activity and soul. Nature consists in the spontaneity of movement, desire; desire implies a final end, a first good which engenders it and attracts it to itself, eternal object of love, immovable in the absolute perfection of its action.

God is Absolute Good, without degrees and without differences; every being receives from Him good with life according to its power. The inequality of beings in their participation of good results from the invincible and fatal necessity of matter. Matter is the potential which includes imperfection. Everything aspires and advances towards Good as its end. In the measure that nature breaks away from the necessity of matter it is less subject to chance and change; its freedom consists in the desire which attracts it towards the good. Evil has its source in potentiality and is only manifested in the development of the opposition which it encloses, an opposition that does not pass beyond the world of contingency and change. The world is not divided between two hostile principles; Absolute Good has no contrary, it is the final end of everything.

The beauty of the world, the harmonious relation of its parts, the glory of the stars and the immutable order of their courses,—all point to a higher Being from whom the uniform motion and intelligent design of the universe proceed. Aristotle compares the relation of God to the universe to that of a general to his army. "The good of an army is in its order, but above all in its chief," he says; "for order is through the chief, and not the chief through order."

God is pure activity, energy itself, prior to potentiality, not according to time, but logically. Time is a subordinate element of that which is universal; the Absolute Essence is timeless. God is in "the eternal heavens," and in the thinking reason of man. He is the final cause whose content is desire and thought. "For the final cause of anything resides in those things of which the one is in existence and the other is not. Now, that which first imparts motion does so as a thing that is loved, and that which has motion impressed upon it imparts motion to other things."

The activity of the divine nature is the activity of pure thought, thought thinking itself. Nature is continually elevating itself from formless matter toward this activity, at every step manifesting more and more clearly the end of its being. The term of its progress is man, a being who thinks, whose intelligence is able to disengage itself little by little from the senses and from imagination until, freed from everything external, it possesses and comprehends itself. The sovereign good for the human soul is pure thought; active intelligence is absolute immateriality.

Potentiality is found in human thinking because it is to a certain extent in a material subject limited by finite conditions. "If a man thinks nothing," Aristotle asks, "what advantage has he over one who sleeps?" If he thinks, and is controlled by another, his thinking is not an activity, but a potentiality. It makes a difference also whether the object of his thought is that which is accidental and transient, or that which is permanent and eternal. In one case the activity is wasted on that which is inferior to itself; in the other the thinking and the object of thought are identical. Thought, therefore, that thinks itself, is the highest and most excellent. It is the absolute final cause, or the Good. It cannot have its object outside of itself; it is not the manifestation of a substance and the product of an activity different from itself.

The essence and the dignity of intelligence lie not in the power, but in the act of thinking. Every good, every perfection, is in action; it is better and sweeter to love than to be loved, to be the subject than the object of thought, better to act than be acted upon. Pure intelligence must be its own object, thought thinking itself, the thought of thought.

For us, as individuals, the activity of pure thinking is permitted only for a short time, and is most excellent: "It is on this account that waking, feeling, thinking, and hopes and memories, produce the richest pleasure." The moments of speculative contemplation in which our thought rediscovers itself in the object of its thought are the ones in which we attain to a feeble conception of divine blessedness. "If God, now, is always in this, as we are at times, then He is admirable; if still more, then more admirable. But He is thus. Life, too, is His; for the actuality of thought is life. He, however, is activity; the activity returning into itself is His most excellent and eternal life. We say, therefore, that God is an eternal and the best life."

All thinking obtains its worth from what is thought; divine thinking can have only the best for its content, and the best is itself. God, therefore, thinks Himself; the energy of thinking and the object which is thought are one and the same; in this consists His absolute perfection and blessedness.

The world is the manifestation of thought, particularized, multiplied, diversified in potentialities of matter which seek to attain reality. On one side we have pure activity, Absolute Being; on the other potentiality, relative being and non-being, existing only in movement, the source of multitude and diversity. Thought is the actuality on which all depends, to which all relates, present to all as the soul to the body, unequally, diversely, according to all possible differences.

But how does God, buried in eternal contemplation of Himself, move the world? How does the pure activity of divine thought enter into relation with nature, matter, potentiality? The divine principle by its essence is separated from potentiality and the instability of movement; it is the end toward which they strive. But whence come the striving, and desire, and movement? How attribute to potentiality any reality?

Aristotle's propositions concerning Deity contain the scientific foundation of theism in philosophy, but they do not escape the difficulty which is the final problem of all theistic speculation—a concept of God in which neither His personality nor essential difference from the finite is lost. God is defined as the

First Mover, Himself unmoved, immaterial, free from all relation to time; but it is difficult to conceive how that which is unmoved can be a moving cause, or how the immaterial can act upon a material universe. The difficulty is partly in our own thinking, for it is certain that a profound insight into the nature of the Divine lies at the basis of Aristotle's philosophy. His God is not mere abstract Being, or dead Identity, but living, eternal Energy. In this principle Greek philosophy reached its culminating point—a principle that finds its justification and complement in the doctrines of Christianity.

CHAPTER XXVII.

ARISTOTLE'S PHYSICS.

ARISTOTLE'S Philosophy of Nature includes its metaphysics in so far as he investigates the problem of existence and the final causes that lie behind sensuous phenomena. This method is rejected by the empirical science of modern times, which holds fast to the facts given in experience, but waives all inquiry into their speculative origin. Aristotle did not neglect the empirical, he sought to make facts the basis of every theory; but his materials were scanty, and he worked without those aids for the advance and verification of science which exist to-day. What he accomplished was wonderful as a mere map of the sciences in the fourth century, B. C. He stated in outline at least the questions which each science must answer, and through his very mistakes cleared the way for their solution. "It is half-way to knowledge when you know what you have to inquire."

His philosophic view of nature was broad and comprehensive. He traced a continuous thread of evolution throughout its ascending scale of life, from the inorganic to the organic, on to the animal, and lastly to man. He considered Nature both as final cause and as necessity. Material causes are only the indispensable condition of natural existence; the true cause is its internal, immanent conformity to design, which constitutes its final end. "That which happens in nature happens always or nearly always the same, but nothing which is through chance or accident reproduces itself. In the next place, that which contains a purpose conforms to this as well in its antecedents as in its consequences; so that the nature of a thing may be inferred from its constitution, and conversely its constitution from its nature; this follows from the idea of design." . . . . "Whoever assumes an accidental origin of things denies, in so doing, nature and the natural order of things; for the natural involves a principle in itself, by means of which a continual progress is made until the attainment of its end and aim." The oak is produced from the acorn, the acorn from the oak; plants produce seed, yet presuppose seed as their own origin. Nature as life is final cause; the living being changes, but preserves itself through its own activity.

Nature is twofold, matter and form, form being the end and aim on account of which all changes occur. The end is not always attained by reason of the obstacles offered by matter. This is the ground of chance and necessity. Nature works according to design, but in its realization produces much from mere necessity. The origin of necessity is sometimes explained "as if one should suppose that a house is through necessity for the reason that the heavy is placed underneath and the light on top, so that the foundations and the rocks are placed lowest and then the earthy matter, and lastly the wood above all because it is the lightest." The material is necessary to the house, but the house is not made for the material, but for shelter and protection.

The necessary in nature is limited to matter and its movements; the final cause is nature's reason and higher principle. Necessity is present in matter, but must be worked upon by the free activity of form in order to constitute natural existence. Chance is a mere exception thwarting the reason which guides and has ever guided the operations of nature. Nature as a whole is a gradual overcoming of matter through form, more and more perfect development of life; what is first in itself is last according to temporal origin, the beginning is also the end.

The universal conditions of natural existence are motion, space, time. Metaphysically, motion is defined as the realizing of that which a thing is potentially. Aristotle illustrates this by saying that metal is the possibility of a statue; but the movement required in it to become a statue is not a movement of the metal as metal, but as this possibility itself. The merely potential whose activity is motion is not self-end, and is therefore imperfect. The mover in the movable is the final cause, the principle and aim of the motion. Activity and passivity are the same in movement, but differ in idea, in so far as one is an activity *in* the moved, the other an activity *by* the mover.

Aristotle distinguishes three kinds of motion: quantitative motion, or increase and decrease; qualitative motion, or alteration; and spatial motion, or change of place, to which the other two if examined closely may be traced back. Quantitative motion, or increase and decrease, presupposes partly a qualitative change, partly a change of place. Qualitative change, or alteration, is possible only through spatial contact, for the passive must be touched by the active. Beginning and ending, as regards the individual thing, coincide partly with combination and separation, partly with the transformation of substances, both of which depend on spatial motion. Only this definite thing begins and ends; absolute beginning and ending would leave no substrate of motion or change. Becoming presupposes and is preceded by being, and must be conceived as a transition from the possible to the real, as development.

The concept of space with Aristotle is neither the form nor the limit of individual bodies; if it were, bodies would move *with* space, and not *in* space. It is not the matter of bodies, nor the distance between them, but rather the boundary of the enclosing body against the enclosed. "There is nothing external to the universe, all is contained in the heavens; for the world is the whole. But place is not the heavens; it is only the outermost limits at rest which touch moving bodies. Therefore the earth is in water, the water in air, the air in ether, the ether in the heavens."

Time is not motion although related to it; motion is sometimes slower, sometimes swifter, while time is ever the same. Whatever is determined by the now we call time; it is the measure of movement in respect of the before and after. It is a continuous as well as a discrete quantity, continuous in so far as this present now is the same as in the past; discrete in so far as its being changes every moment. The past and the future are different from the now, but it is their limit; it is both their union and their distinction.

Aristotle maintains that motion is without beginning or end, and from this concept derives his theory of the universe. The absolute motion is circular, without antithesis, uniform, self-complete. God moves the world from its circumference, acting directly on the firmament of the fixed stars. Each motion of a surrounding sphere is communicated to those included in it, but the degree of perfection varies as they are more or less removed from the direct influence of the divine Mover.

Aristotle calls the sphere of the fixed stars "the first Heaven." As nearest God it consists not of perishable matter, but of imperishable ether, the divine element in creation. Its motion is the pure circular, unbecome, unchangeable, that from which all other motion springs. Touched by no earthly trouble, comprehending all space and all time, the fixed stars rejoice as the most perfect of created beings.

Lower than the stars is the sphere of the planets, including the sun and the moon. Lowest of all is the earth, the farthest removed from God and therefore the most imperfect of created things. This is the sphere of movement in a straight line, upward, downward, as the elements are heavy or light. Earth, water, air, fire, all pass over into each other and form one whole, a circle whose parts ceaselessly change but the law of whose process is uniform and eternal, exhibiting thus a copy of heaven. "That which is changed in things, is only the sensuously perceivable; and the forms and shapes, as well as the properties, are not changed; they originate and vanish in things, but do not change."

Life consists in the power of self-motion, in the capability of a being to produce a change in itself even though that change be limited to growth, nourishment and decay. That which is moved in the living is its body, or matter; that which moves is its soul, or form, called by Aristotle entelechy. He distinguishes in theory at least, between entelechy and energy; entelechy contains the end (telos) of a process, and is not only form, but principle of motion and final end. The body exists for the soul, and the soul is the true explanation of body. Soul gives reality to body just as vision gives reality to the eye. "We must no more ask whether the soul and the body are one than ask whether the wax and the figure impressed upon it are one, or generally inquire whether the material and that of which it is the material, are one." Only through the soul can we comprehend the body; the mental functions, although the outcome of the physical, are the presupposition on which they rest.

As the entelechy of body, soul is its perfect realization; but this realization is not necessarily explicit, it may be implicit. Aristotle, therefore, defines soul as the "first entelechy" of body. He recognizes three stages in its development, the vegetative, the sensitive, and the intellectual soul, corresponding to the life of plants, of animals, and of man. His psychology rests upon the biological conception of a progressive development of life on earth. Man is the end of creation, the perfect development of all that is contained implicitly and imperfectly in lower forms of existence. The inorganic precedes the organic; the functions of nutrition are the basis for the faculties of sense; the exercise of the senses is necessary to provide material for thought.

We must not neglect the distinction between what is prior in time and prior in order of thought. Aristotle repeatedly asserts that as the idea of reality precedes that of potentiality, the more developed form stands first in thought and real being, although the lower form has the priority in time. Soul is the unity which embraces life, sense-perception, and thought; it is the true universal, containing within itself the individual and the particular. It is not abstract but concrete unity, developing and annulling its own multiplicity, as vegetative, sensitive, intellectual, reaching a higher and higher synthesis in its progress towards perfect realization.

Among living beings plants are the lowest. The work of the vegetative soul is reduced to two functions, nutrition and reproduction. It is related to matter in a material manner, employing it as nutriment; it has nothing to do with the form of the object as in sensation. "The reaction of the life of the plant upon the external world is not sufficient to constitute a fixed, abiding individuality." says Dr. Wm. T. Harris, in an article on "Educational Psychology," published in *The Journal of Speculative Philosophy*: "With each accretion there is some change of particular individuality. Every growth to a plant is by the sprouting out of new individuals—new plants—a ceaseless multiplication of individuals, and not the preservation of the same individual. The species is preserved, but not the particular individual. Each limb, each twig, even each new leaf is a new individual, which grows out from the previous growth as the first sprout grew from the seed. Each part furnishes a soil for the next. When a plant no longer sends out new individuals, we say it is dead. The life of the plant is only a life of nutrition."

We reach a higher grade of life in the faculties of sense which first constitute the animal. Sense receives the form of things and is so far passive, acted upon from without ; but to produce sensation it must in its turn act upon and assimilate this passive content. "The sensible object is not so much the condition as the occasion of sensation," says Mr. Wallace, in his introduction to Aristotle's De Anima. "Perception is something internal and immanent, only called out into action by an external object. . . . To Aristotle, therefore, we may say that matter is not a permanent possibility of sensation realized in perception but sensation a permanent possibility of perceiving what as perceived is the realization of the sensitive capacities."

Aristotle explains the general character of sense-perception by comparing it to the manner in which wax receives the form or impress of the seal, but not its material, the iron or the gold of which it is composed. This does not mean that the soul like wax has no form or activity in itself ; it is simply a metaphor to illustrate that what is sensuously perceived in so far as it is form is the object as universal, not as individual.

Touch is the most common of the perceptive faculties; it is the sense which all others presuppose. Touch and taste contribute only to our animal existence; sight and hearing are directed to our spiritual development. The heart rather than the brain is the seat of sensation. This evidently means that it is through the heart that the soul compares and distinguishes sensations; to interpret it otherwise would contradict Aristotle's theory of the relation between mind and matter.

Imagination (*Vorstellung*), the picture-making faculty, is closely connected with sensation. But its testimony is less trustworthy. As a copy of early impressions we call it remembrance; as their conscious reproduction we call it re-collection. Re-collection implies reason, and belongs to man alone. The laws according to which the mind works in this process are those of the Association of Ideas, which is one of Aristotle's contributions to mental science.

Man includes in himself the vegetative soul of the plant, the sensitive soul of the animal, and the cognitive soul, or the power of thinking, which distinguishes him from all other beings. The soul in itself is the divine in man, independent of bodily conditions, immaterial, self-subsistent. But so far as it is related to sensation it is passively determined, and is in a process of development. Aristotle, therefore, distinguishes between what he calls the active and the passive reason, a distinction whose interpretation has given rise to wide divergencies of view among Aristotelian scholars. On one hand he could not overlook the gradual development of spiritual activities; on the other he could not think pure reason as connected in any way with matter. This antithesis in the soul of man he sought to explain and reconcile by means of his theory, and considering the difficulty of the problem it is little wonder that his meaning is sometimes obscure.

Reason contains within itself potentially the general concepts by which a world of sense becomes a world for intellect; it needs only to develop these from itself in order to apply them to experience. "The process of thought is like that of writing on a writing-tablet on which nothing is yet actually written," says Aristotle. This does not mean that thought is the product of the external world, or that it is like a writing-tablet in passivity, since the activity of thought is not external to but within itself. The figure must not be taken in its whole extent; interpreted in the light of other passages it implies that the soul has a content only in so far as it is really thought, that the potentiality within it must become actuality through its own activity.

"Now in the case of immaterial objects, the subject thinking and the object thought are one and the same," says Aristotle; "just as speculative science is equivalent to the objects and ideas of speculative knowledge. In the case, on the contrary, of those objects which are imbedded in matter, each of the ideas of reason is present, if only potentially and implicitly. And thus reason is not to be regarded as belonging to and governed by the things of sense, but the world of thought must be regarded as belonging to and regulated by reason.

. . . . This reason is, on the one hand, of such a character as to *become* all things; on the other hand of such a nature as to *create* all things, acting then much in the same way as some positive quality, such as for instance light; for light also in a way creates actual out of potential color. . . . And thus, though knowledge as an actually realized condition is identical with its object, this knowledge as a potential capacity is in time prior to the individual, though in universal existence it is not even in time thus prior to actual thought. . . . . This phase of reason is separated from and uncompounded with material conditions, and, being in its essential character fully and actually realized, it is not subject to impressions from without, for the creative is in every case more knowable than the passive, just as the originating principle is superior to the matter which it forms."

"The first key to understanding Aristotle is to know that *dunamis* and *energeia* are relative terms," says Mr. Wallace, "and that what is an *energeia* from one aspect may be a *dunamis* from another. And thus Aristotle may perfectly well say that the different forms of soul must exist in man potentially before they can do so actually and yet hold that it is in potential forms that reason as an actual or rather as an actualizing faculty is present originally in man."

Aristotle's theory of knowledge determines directly

his theory of practical activity. What in the one sphere is truth and error, is in the other good and evil; "it is when the sense perceives something as pleasant or painful that the mind affirms or denies it, that it pursues it or avoids it."

Desire arises from sensuous feeling, but assumes a different character according as it is or is not dominated by reason. So far as desire is influenced by reason, reason is practical, and desire itself becomes will. Between the two stands the human soul with freedom of choice, spontaneity of action. The difficulties that lie in the concept of the freedom of the will did not exist for Aristotle. He looked upon reason as the basis of the moral and the intellectual life. Man even in yielding to his animal nature is conscious of a higher ideal; this consciousness presupposes reason whose essence is freedom.

Aristotle's theory of reason has puzzled both ancient and modern commentators. The active or the creative reason transcends the body, is eternal and imperishable, unaffected by matter, prior and subsequent to the individual mind; the passive or receptive reason is necessary to individual thought, but is subjected to suffering and change, and therefore perishable. Where is the personal self to be found, in the active or in the passive reason? Did Aristotle believe in the immortality of the individual soul?

Hegel thinks that Aristotle reached the highest point of speculation in identifying the subjective and the objective present in active or creative reason, but separated in finite things and finite mind where reason is only a potentiality. As this unity of subjective and objective, reason must be self-consciousness. It is the true totality, the activity which is both in itself and for itself, the thinking of thinking, that which constitutes the nature of Absolute Spirit, and in so far as we participate in it it is the consciousness of God, perfect blessedness.

CHAPTER XXVIII.

ARISTOTLE'S ETHICS.

WHAT is the chief good for man?—is the question asked and answered by Aristotle in his Ethics. As physical things strive unconsciously towards completion and perfection, man consciously seeks the good attainable in life. This good, according to Aristotle, is happiness, which can only be realized in the harmonious activity and development of his especial nature. It differs from physical good in so far as it exists not only *for* man, but *in* man. The end of the physical is an end not recognized by the physical itself, the end of the moral is consciously recognized and realized. Aristotle, in his Ethics, views the final cause subjectively as happiness; objectively, as the morally beautiful.

The activity which results in happiness belongs to man as man, not as animal; it is the activity of reason. It is not mere sensuous enjoyment, but the chief human good, containing in itself all that lends to life its highest worth. It is not selfish except in that higher sense of the word where egoism becomes altruism, and genuine self-culture humanitarianism. It even rises above the practical sphere of morality, in its highest realization; it is that for which morality exists, the divine in man, a state of peace and blessedness, the summit of human perfection.

Aristotle views happiness from the external as well as the internal point of view. Ideal happiness is the attainment of a state wherein man would live above the world, participating in the blessed life of God. But moral activity is human activity, the activity of beings limited by time and space. Aristotle, therefore, regards happiness as partly dependent on certain external advantages, health, moderate means, friends, children, etc. He was led to this second view by his empirical tendencies and the facts to which universal experience seemed to testify. "The work of man is a conscious and active life of the soul in accordance with reason," he says: "this is the virtuous and therefore the happy life." Happiness implies virtue and a life favorably situated as regards external fortune; but it depends on mental rather than on bodily conditions, and is an activity or *energeia* as distinguished from *dunamis* or potentiality.

"No conception equally plastic with *energeia*, and at all answering to it, can be found in modern thought," says Sir Alexander Grant. "Energy, as we use the word, does not convey the meaning fully; nor does actuality, which gives more nearly its philosophical import. To comprehend *energeia*, we must study its various applications in Aristotle's system of philosophy. It is everywhere the correlative and opposite of *dunamis*."

We have seen its significance in physics; in ethics, it is not only identified with happiness, but expresses moral action and the development of the moral powers. The moral *dunamis*, or potentiality, differs from the physical; it is not restricted to one of two contraries which it must produce, as the capacity of heat produces heat alone, but it can develop into either contrary and is therefore freed from physical necessity. The moral *dunamis* is not a gift of nature independent of any effort on our part; it does not exist previous to moral action. It arises gradually through exercise: good acts produce good habits, and conversely good habits produce good acts.

If man had a capacity for virtue as irresistible as the force which makes the stone fall to the ground, he would have no choice, no responsibility, no morality. All men are born with certain capacities of growth, of feeling pleasure and pain; but to acquire the disposition of virtue we must first of all be virtuous. This seems paradoxical, but Aristotle compares the acts by which we acquire virtue to the first attempts of the artist in the acquirement of his art. They are merely external and lack morality until they express internal and developed character.

Man is a free and intelligent agent, according to Aristotle, accountable for his good or evil action. The basis of morality is found in natural tendencies, but morality itself consists in their transformation through rational insight and will. Aristotle reversed the proposition of Socrates that no one is voluntarily bad, finding in the will itself the decisive proof of moral choice and responsibility. Virtue is an enduring quality of the will acquired only through continued virtuous activity; that which was first a matter of free choice becomes a permanent element of character.

If we ask what quality of the will is virtuous, Aristotle answers that moral activity must observe the just mean between the too-much and the too-little, must avoid both excess and defect. This thought is essentially Greek; it is the law of moderation applied to moral action. What is too much for one man may not be for another; the virtue of a free man is one thing, that of a slave another. The external circumstances and moral problems of individuals differ and thus determine their virtue. Whenever there is uncertainty the mean to be observed is decided by practical insight.

Virtue is a certain harmony of life. In so far as it is connected with the control of the passions it is moral; in so far as it is connected with the order of the intellect it is intellectual, or *dianœtic*. Moral virtue includes courage, temperance, generosity, courtesy, loftiness of spirit, and chief of all, justice. Courage is the mean between rashness and cowardice; temperance is the mean between sensuality and asceticism; generosity is the mean between avarice and prodigality. Justice, finally, is the mean between the doing of wrong and the suffering of wrong, between selfishness and weakness. Upon justice rests the maintenance of the community. It is therefore the connecting link between ethics and politics. All the passions tend toward excess, but guided by reason they are the springs that move the world, the source of human greatness.

Intellectual virtue is prudence, good sense, practical wisdom. It is our duty to acquire knowledge that knowledge may guide and mould our conduct. Virtue and insight condition each other; one gives to the will the direction towards the good, the other defines the good. In intellectual, or *dianœtic* virtue, ethics finds its complement in philosophy.

Aristotle's theory that the distinction between virtue and vice is merely quantitative has been greatly criticized in modern times. It contains truth, and expresses the Greek idea of virtue as beauty in action. But it leaves unexpressed the law of right binding on the moral subject, the conception of duty. "To some extent this is supplied by Aristotle's doctrine of the *telos*," say Sir Alexander Grant, "which raises a beautiful action into something absolutely desirable, and makes it the end of our being."

Another point that has been frequently discussed in Aristotle's ethics is the relation of happiness to self-consciousness. The idea of consciousness is implied in the ethical application of *energeia*; *energeia* exists not only *for* the mind, but *in* the mind; it is not only life, but the sense of life; not only thought, but the consciousness of thought. Nevertheless we must not identify *energeia* as applied to the mind with self-consciousness; one is an ancient, the other a modern term, implying in part but not wholly the same idea.

Aristotle regards the chief good as existing in man and for man, in the development and fruition of his own powers. Let him "energize," "actualize" that which is potential or latent in his own nature, and the result is happiness. Virtue must be active, not passive: positive, not negative. It is the *doing of right,* which is very different from the *not doing of wrong.*

The general striving for pleasure is the impulse of life itself. The nobler an activity the higher the pleasure united with its exercise; the source of the purest enjoyment is thinking and moral action. Pleasure is not to be the aim and motive of our acts, but only a result. It is associated with virtue in so far as virtuous activity is self-satisfaction. True self-love consists in striving to be intelligent, loving, helpful, in the highest sense. It is better to suffer than to do injustice, because in one case the injury is external, in the other internal. Even life itself is but the means to a higher end when it is sacrificed by the brave man for friends and country.

Pleasure differs from happiness in so far as happiness is essentially moral and ideal, extending over an entire life; whereas reality and brevity of duration belong to pleasure. The one is a blessed state of the internal life; the other depends on favorable external circumstances. But in so far as pleasure consists in the exercise of the highest faculties it is identical with happiness. For happiness is not a means to something else but the end in itself, the morally worthy in which the mind rests self-satisfied.

In his classification of the virtues, Aristotle omits the Christian graces,—charity, humility, self-renunciation. He separates ethics from religion, and does not consider man's relation to God except so far as it is included in man's relation to his fellow-men. The highest virtue is dianoetic rather than ethical, an excellence of the intellect to which the doctrine of the mean is inapplicable.

Wisdom is what is best and noblest, and its attainment is the supreme degree of felicity.

Friendship is treated by Aristotle as "either a virtue, or closely connected with virtue;" it is the middle term which leads from ethics to politics. "Now to the solitary individual life is grievous; for it is not easy to maintain a glow of mind by one's self, but in company with some one else, and in relation to others, this is easier." A friend intensifies the sense of personal existence, the vitality on which happiness depends. Friendship is the bond that unites man to man, not merely externally, as community of right, but in the innermost essence of his being. True friendship is wholly disinterested. It widens the morality of the individual, but is an association limited by accidental personal relations. The state embraces a larger circle, and here first in its laws and institutions morality finds a permanent basis; ethics rests upon politics.

CHAPTER XXIX.

ARISTOTLE'S POLITICS, PHILOSOPHY OF ART, ETC.

THE state, according to Aristotle, is as essential to man's existence as the act of birth; without it his potentialities as a spiritual being could not be realized. He defines man as a political animal, destined by nature for association with others. The state is the condition of moral perfection; it is the moral whole whose basis is the family, and though later in temporal development is in itself prior to the family and the individual, as the whole is prior to the part. Cut off from the social community man is either "a god or a beast." It is the state that reveals and actualizes his own better self; it is at once the back-ground and the result of his special activities. Politics, therefore, is the indispensable presupposition and completion of ethics.

The aim of the state is not merely the physical welfare of its citizens, but their virtuous activity and consequent happiness. The state comprehends in itself all moral aims; it must secure by its institutions the best life for man, and that life is best which unites theoretical and practical activity.

According to temporal origin the family must precede the state as the condition of its beginning. The family exists in a threefold relation, the relation of husband to wife, of parents to children, of master to slave. Aristotle treats marriage as a moral relation, but looks upon the wife as rightly dependent upon her husband, because woman is inferior to man in strength of character. That is, he regards woman as passive rather than active, and therefore inferior to man. She is so far free that she has her own domestic sphere in which the husband must not interfere.

A relation of greater dependence is that of children to parents; one of complete dependence is that of slave to master. Aristotle regards slavery as necessary in order to give the master leisure to lead a noble life. He would base it on superiority of virtue alone. It is fitting that those who are capable of spiritual activity should command and guide those who are not; the relation is beneficial both to master and slave. Aristotle defends slavery, but would change its character. Underlying his sanction of it as an institution is the idea that he who is by nature a slave will be enslaved. In order to be free man must develop his own internal activity and make himself independent of everything external. The political slave may be the freeman. Aristotle overlooks the truth that to hold one in bondage is not to encourage the desire for spiritual growth and excellence. He held that a slave might earn his freedom by showing himself worthy of it, and went so far practically as to free his own slaves. But he regarded society without slavery something as we should view it to-day without domestic service. The Greek thought did not recognize the essential freedom of man as man. It made clear one side of the truth, the objective freedom of the state, but neglected the other, the subjective freedom of the individual.

Aristotle had the Greek prejudice against trade and traffic. He draws a sharp distinction between necessary and noble work. He asserts that commodities are made for man, not man for the multiplication of commodities. He undervalues work for pecuniary gain, and does not believe in lending money on interest.

Aristotle does not share Plato's communistic views. His arguments are nearly the same as those of modern opponents. The state like the body of man has many members and cannot be reduced to an unmeaning unity, a levelling process that in destroying difference would destroy the organism. Communism would impoverish human life, render impossible those virtues which consist in a right relation to possessions, rob men of opportunities of virtuous action, and diminish happiness.

Aristotle recognizes not only the industrial value of the institution of private property, but the part it plays in the subjugation of nature by man. Considered as representing this subjugation by free individuals, differing in gifts and capacities, or as a means for their fulfillment of social functions, property must be unequal. Men cannot have all things in common, but they can have more in common than at present. The instinct of ownership is implanted by nature, but should be tempered by liberality and benevolence. The legislator should seek to inspire the love which is the fulfilling of the law, but should not take away the freedom of virtuous action on the part of the individual. Prof. Jowett has thrown the ancient thought into this modern form: "More good will be done by awakening in rich men a sense of the duties of property than by the violation of its rights."

"We see in this contrast to Platonic Socialism," says Zeller, "not only the practical sense of Aristotle, his clear glance open to the conditions and laws of reality, his horror of all ethical one-sidedness, his deep understanding of human nature and the life of the state, but also, as in Plato, the connection of his political views with the metaphysical basis of his system." Plato would have cancelled private possessions and destroyed individual interests, because he recognized the Idea only in the Universal, the State as the substance of the Individual; Aristotle, on the other hand, regarded the Individual as essentially the Universal. The activity which seeks the welfare of the state must proceed from individuals and their free will; only from within through culture and education, not from without through compulsory institutions of Socialism or Communism, can the life of the state be maintained and preserved.

Aristotle's ideal state is an organism of limited size, a body of men not too large nor too small, able to rule and be ruled with a view to the common advantage, the realization of the highest type of life. Every citizen is to be a landowner, but no great accumulation of property is to be allowed. The essential aim of the state is the moral perfection of its citizens, whose result is happiness. Those who contribute to this most have the justest claim to political influence. With the Greek scorn of manual labor and trade, agriculturists, artisans, and tradesmen are excluded from the rights and duties of citizenship. The attainment of virtue and happiness by the higher natures has its accompanying shadow; it implies the existence and recognized inferiority of the lower. Only the few inherit the earth, but the condition of this inheritance with Aristotle is an active life of moral and intellectual greatness. So far as any individual or class of citizens contribute to the existence of the state and the common good of the whole, just so far should their influence extend. The few are to elevate the masses, and develop in all the best type of life of which they are capable.

The state is both an outcome of the past and a reflection of the present; its constitution is its mode of life, varying with varying circumstances, but exerting always an ethical influence over character. The happiness which is its aim consists essentially in the virtue of its citizens, a work of conscious activity, of free-will and of insight. The state must therefore educate its citizens, men must be formed who know how to exercise the virtue of the free. Education must develop the whole man, physical, intellectual, moral. Its aim should be spiritual rather than material, culture rather than utility; the development of the lower nature should be adjusted to the ultimate development of that which is highest in man. Education must tend not only towards practical activity, but to a right use of leisure. Some things are to be learned for practical activity; others on their own account. The one has an aim outside of itself in something to be attained; the other in its exercise is a beautiful and satisfying activity. To be always seeking the useful does not become free and exalted minds. Both Plato and Aristotle believe that school is the place for inspiring a love of all that is noble and beautiful rather than for pouring in knowledge. Let one first learn to love what is right, then learn why it is right. Aristotle declines to give a direct training to the intellect until he has first laid a solid foundation of character. He postpones the appeal to reason that it may be the more effectual when it is made. To be educated in the best sense is to be rational.

Greek education differed from modern education in placing a higher value on a general aptitude of knowing, an interest in human relations generally, than on special acquirements which may be one-sided and tend towards work in a groove. Gymnastics, music and literature were its chief branches. The aim of gymnastics with Aristotle was not so much technical skill as to lay the foundations of a harmoniously developed being, healthy and undisturbed in body and mind. So, too, with music; its chief value for Aristotle was its power to influence the character and mould it to virtue. Music inclines the child through his emotions to take pleasure in the good, and to reject what is evil, disposing the soul to virtue. For we are not really virtuous, according to Aristotle, until we love virtue for its own sake.

The high place assigned to music by the Greeks is one that we can only partly comprehend; to their thought it produced an elevation of the soul by harmonizing all its discordant elements. Through its influence man was lifted above himself, and "caught up into a sort of heaven." There must have been in Greek music some spiritual union of mind and sense which found a way to the inner place of the soul, experienced by us only in rare moments.

The aim of Aristotle's education is to develop a many-sided moral being, capable of fulfilling the duties of the perfect citizen, and of playing different parts, as soldier, statesman, judge, philosopher. Not wise laws, but wise men, are the basis of his state; men who will always prefer virtue to wealth and distinction. The best state is a brotherhood of men, limited it is true to a few chosen ones of the Greek race, but animated by the noble purpose of living and helping each other to live a life of virtue. Man must join with his fellows and live for their welfare as well as his own in order to realize himself as a spiritual being. Society must elevate and ennoble, not warp and distort the individual. For this the state exists, and not for empire or wealth. Its end is spiritual, not material. Men are always losing sight of the true and the good in the pursuit of material interest. To correct this tendency, ethics must be infused into politics. The ultimate identification of the two by the greatest thinkers of Greece, is a truth to be constantly enforced.

PHILOSOPHY OF ART.

Aristotle's theory of art is found in his Poetics, a little work devoted chiefly to the discussion of tragedy. He places art as a means of spiritual enjoyment in the most intimate connection with spiritual development. The aim of tragedy is to purify the emotions of pity and fear, to make men see life in its true light. Purification (Katharsis) is a quieting produced through excitement, a homœopathic healing. How is it effected? Not as in real life, where the single thing ruled by accident is placed before the eyes, but by showing us the universal in the single, the common human lot guided by the law of eternal justice. The fate in tragedy must be self-deserved; a work of art must disclose the unchanging order of the moral universe. In this lies its power to purge the mind of the sensuous, "enabling us to see reality truly and correctly," comprehending its spiritual purpose and significance.

THE PERIPATETIC SCHOOL.

Theophrastus, Eudemus and Strabo are the most famous leaders of the school of Aristotle, called the Peripatetic. Theophrastus was his immediate successor, but seems like the others to have been little more than a commentator. There was so much to expound and elaborate in Aristotle's system of thought that we find in his disciples a lack of independent research and originality. Their work, therefore, is of but slight importance. The early loss of Aristotle's writings may have led to their misinterpretation; various theories, inconsistent with their spirit, were handed down traditionally.

CHAPTER XXX.

TRANSITION TO THE POST-ARISTOTELIAN PHILOSOPHY.

ARISTOTLE was both a scientist and a philosopher. He therefore sought in his system of thought to unite the most comprehensive observation with the dialectic development of the concept. The school of Socrates and Plato neglected the outer world of experience for the inner world of thought; Aristotle recognized that thought is not independent of experience, although it is that only which is known, the essence, the form of things, their immanent idea. His system thus completes and contradicts the Platonic, as Zeller observes; completes it in so far as he maintains the reality of thought alone, contradicts it in so far as he places its activity within and not outside of matter. Matter is the not-yet-being of form, the potential; form is the actual. The relation between the two is positive instead of negative, producing motion and life, becoming and change. The presupposition of this relation is pure form, a self-mover, self-thinking Reason.

Greek philosophy reaches its culminating point in the clear enunciation of this principle, although it is not able to escape dualism in its application. How is matter, the potential, derived from and related to pure form, pure actuality, pure thought? How can the circle of the known world of experience be explained and comprehended as an organization of self-thinking thought? This is the problem.

The idea with Aristotle is thought as the unity of the subjective and the objective, the true universal. But it is applied dogmatically in the systems of Stoicism and Epicureanism; sceptically, in Scepticism and the New Academy; mystically, in Neo-Platonism. All these systems neglect the objective and emphasize the subjective. The essential being of man, according to Aristotle, is reason; its highest activity is pure thinking, which turns away from everything external to employ itself with concepts alone. It is only a step farther in this direction to turn away entirely from the external world to the internal world of consciousness. This step was taken by the post-Aristotelians; with all their contradictions they agree in this common feature of abstract subjectivity. The Stoics, the Epicureans, and the Sceptics all agree in preferring the practical to the theoretical interest, and in seeking its satisfaction in mental serenity and independence.

The philosophy of Greece was closely connected with her political life. Nothing remained after her loss of independence but to oppose one's inner self to her hopeless condition and seek contentment in the recesses of the soul. The need of the time was not so much theoretical knowing as moral strength. The apathy of the Stoics, the self-contentment of the Epicureans, the equanimity of the Sceptics, reflected the spirit of the age. When, too, the barriers were broken down that separated the West from the East, the Greek from the barbarian, **man** became conscious that moral life is a relation of man to man independent of nationality, and this consciousness found expression in philosophy.

The deepening of self-consciousness, characteristic of post-Aristotelian philosophy, is expressed one-sidedly as the abstract universality of thought—Stoicism, or as the abstract individuality of feeling—Epicureanism, or as the negation of this one-sidedness—Scepticism. Stoicism seeks happiness by suppressing all selfish feelings and inclinations, subordinating the individual to the law of the whole; Epicureanism, in the absence of suffering, painlessness, imperturbability. Finally, Scepticism concludes from the contradictory systems of thought that knowledge is impossible, and deduces from this conclusion serene indifference towards everything. All three strive towards the same end, though in different ways; the internal freedom of self-consciousness, imperturbability of spirit, abstract independence.

Transplanted to Roman soil in the first century B.C., Greek philosophy, especially Stoicism and Epicureanism, found many adherents. Touched by the Roman breadth of empire and the Roman spirit, it became eclectic in character, and wholly practical in its aim. The Roman world was the world of abstraction, crushing out and deadening all spiritual beauty and spontaneity. Hence its need in philosophy to tear itself loose from the external and find within the soul the freedom it could not otherwise enjoy.

In Alexandria, the West and the East touched each other in deep and lasting contact. Here Greek philosophy came to a close in Neo-Platonism—a final attempt to solve the dualism between the subjective and the objective. Neo-Platonism with all its differences bears the same character of subjectivity as the earlier systems of Stoicism, Epicureanism, and Scepticism. Its great aim is to mediate between God and man, to exalt the individual subject to the Absolute Subject, not through knowledge, but through ecstasy—a divine illumination of the soul.

CHAPTER XXXI.

STOICISM.

ZENO, the founder of the Stoic School, was born about the year 340 B. C., in Citium, a town of Asia Minor. His father was a Phœnician merchant who in his frequent trips to Athens collected a large number of the writings of the philosophers, especially of the Socratists. Their perusal awakened in Zeno the love of knowledge, and the resolve to dedicate his life to its pursuit. It is said that the loss of his worldly goods in a shipwreck turned his activity from commerce to philosophy, but his character and life prove that inward inclination had more to do with it than outward accident. He removed to Athens and received instruction from Xenocrates, from Crates the Cynic, from Stilpo the Megaric, and from Polemo the Academic. After studying and listening to others for twenty years he opened a school of his own in the *Stoa Poecile*, a portico adorned with paintings of Polygnotus, whence the name "Philosophers of the Porch," or "Stoics." He taught here for fifty-eight years, and then in undisturbed health ended his life voluntarily. He was greatly honored by the Athenians for his simplicity and temperance and the strictness of his morality. On the monument to his memory, erected at public expense, was this inscription: "His life corresponded to his precepts."

Zeno's successor in the Stoa was Cleanthes, a native of Asia Minor. When summoned by the Athenian court to give an account of his manner of life, he testified that he carried water for a gardener nightly that he might devote his days to the study of philosophy.

Cleanthes was followed by Chrysippus of Cilicia, who is sometimes considered the second founder of Stoic philosophy, because he so elaborated and extended its doctrines. He is said to have written daily five hundred lines and to have composed seven hundred and five books. This is not so wonderful as it seems when we consider that his works were partly compilations and repetitions of doctrines previously enunciated. Not a single one remains, but it would be hard to choose between their utter loss and the preservation of all.

Other celebrated Stoics are Zeno of Tarsus, Diogenes the Babylonian, Posidonius of Rhodes, and Panætius, the principal disseminator of Stoicism in Rome. These later teachers blended other doctrines with their Stoicism, and proceeded eclectically. The most celebrated Roman Stoics are Seneca, the slave Epictetus of Phrygia, and the Emperor Marcus Aurelius.

The essential aim of philosophy with the Stoics is the exercise, the learning of virtue. The centre of human activity and striving is the moral life. Physics, according to Chrysippus, is only necessary because it gives us a means of deciding concerning good and evil, what we shall do and what we shall avoid. Philosophy is itself a virtue and guides us to right acting. The virtuous man is he who subordinates himself to the laws of the universe. To do this he must know the laws;

virtue is knowledge with the Stoics, as with Socrates. They insist on strength of will, but strength of will is inseparably united with right knowledge. Philosophy is in the closest union with practical life; it is not merely a virtue, but without it virtue is impossible.

The Stoics divide philosophy into logic, physics, and ethics. Logic is an outwork of the system, the method for attaining true knowledge. Ethics is the final aim of philosophic activity, the guidance to virtue; but virtue consists in subordinating one's self to the eternal order of the universe, investigated by physics. The study of physics or logic, outside of their significance for ethics, is superfluous.

THE LOGIC OF THE STOICS.

The Stoics regard sensuous perception as the original source of all our knowledge; the soul is a blank until written upon by impressions from the outside world. Sensuous perception of itself is not knowledge; to it must be added the activity of the understanding. But the understanding has no other matter except that which is given to it by sensuous perception. Zeno compared sensation to the outstretched fingers; assent, as the first mental activity, to the closed hand; conception to the fist; and knowledge to one fist firmly grasped by the other. The difference between sensation and knowledge is in the greater or less strength of conviction; it is merely subjective and gradual—one of degree, not of kind.

The bulwark against doubt is practical need; knowledge must be possible, or man could not act morally. The criterion of truth is the concept which produces in the mind immediate certainty of its correspondence and identity with the object. Hegel praises the insight of the Stoics, the witness of the subjective reason to the objective reasonableness of the world. But he finds the unity which it expresses merely formal because it does not contain difference as well as identity. The true criterion is thought as self-determination, developing and at the same time annulling its own antithesis of subjective and objective.

The Stoics contradict themselves—seeking on the one hand a solid basis for a scientific process of proof, and on the other turning to the immediate, the sensuous, as the ground of certainty. They lose sight of the especial problem of logic—an exposition of the real laws and operations of thought—to busy themselves with empty forms and abstractions. The chief value of their work lies in their recognition of the principle that the universal as thought is the true universal, although they are not able to show its self-separation and self-identification in the particular and the individual.

THE PHYSICS OF THE STOICS.

The Stoics assert that nothing exists except the corporeal, widening its concept so as to include the soul, virtue, truth, God. According to Plato a man is just when he participates in the idea of justice; according to the Stoics a man is just when he has in him the material producing justice. This materialism is not wholly consistent inasmuch as they do not deny the existence and incorporeality of thought, or space, or time. It seems foreign to the ideal moral tendencies of their philosophy, but is nevertheless grounded in its practical character.

Their point of view is that of ordinary common sense which knows of nothing real except the sensible and the corporeal. What they seek to discover is a firm basis for human activity. In action man is brought into direct contact with the external world, and its existence is taken for granted. Hence the Stoics infer that the only reality is that which acts upon us or is acted upon by us, the corporeal. It follows from this that the individual perception is alone true; and yet the Stoics inconsistently ascribe higher truth to the general concept.

Their view of nature is dynamic. They separate the moment of activity from that of passivity; the concept of force is higher than that of matter. Matter alone is real, but the characteristic of reality is causation, capacity to act and be acted upon. Matter cannot move except as it is penetrated by force; force is the energy of God, the soul of the world. Matter and force, the passive and the active, are manifestations of one and the same Being. The second is not independent of the first as with Aristotle, but the two are inseparable. God and the world are identical; the world is God, God is the world. The Stoics will not admit any distinction between the two, hence their pantheism. The spiritual to them is always clothed in the sensuous; God is represented ideally as the Providence of the world, caring for all his creatures; as the perfect, gracious, all-knowing Reason, living a life of eternal blessedness; but he is also Fire, Ether, Air, the Breath, Nature, Destiny, the Whole and the Law of the

Whole. He is the Universal Substance changing into definite forms of matter, whose divine life is an eternal circular process, flowing out into the world to return into itself again. However regarded, as including everything or but a part of real existence, He is indissolubly united with the corporeal.

Following Heraclitus the Stoics believed that the world originated from primitive fire, changing into air, then into earth and water. Everything results from a natural and inflexible connection of causes and effects, otherwise the Divine Force that rules the world would not be its Absolute Cause. This necessity as the law of Nature is Destiny; as the ground of development according to design, Providence. Matter is in constant transition, but the law within it, its formative energy, never changes. This energy, this divine activity, is directed immediately to the whole; mediately to the individual, a part of the whole.

The Stoics affirm a certain freedom of the will, although according to their theory the actions and destinies of men must be predetermined. The law that works in the whole works differently according as its material is inorganic, or organic, or intelligent and reasonable. Our action may be due to our own impulse and decision, although determined by forces that lie in the nature of the universe and of our character. It is so far free as it springs from our will co-operating with external causes; upon this depends moral responsibility. The soul cannot escape the divine law of its being; its freedom consists in being determined, not from without but from within, through its own nature. It is the soul itself that turns to truth or error; intellectual conviction as well as moral action result from and are due to the exercise of our will. What proceeds from my will is my deed, whether it is or is not possible for me to think and act differently. I can obey the law of the whole willingly or unwillingly, freely or under compulsion.

The whole is perfect; whence come imperfection and evil? The Stoics like other philosophers find their justification difficult. Moral evil is the only real evil, and is referred to a necessity of human nature which in order to be human could not be created differently. Evil will in the long run be turned to good, on whose account it exists as a means of development and realization.

The human soul is described as vital warmth diffused throughout the body which it sustains and holds together. It is related to the soul of the world as the part to the whole, and will be absorbed into the Universal Reason, of which it is a dependent portion, at the end of the world-process.

It is difficult to understand how a philosophy like Stoicism, whose chief characteristic is its moral tendency, could deny the freedom of the will and the immortality of the soul. But the same position is taken by a great modern thinker, Spinoza. Doubtless they discerned some kind of unity underneath the contradictory aspects which the problem presents to our limited vision.

THE ETHICS OF THE STOICS.

The central point of Stoicism and its chief glory is ethics. The highest good can only be found in that which is conformable to nature, and nothing is conformable to nature unless it is in harmony with the law of the universe, its divine reason. The reason in man must consciously coöperate with this law, must transform into final cause what is only impulse with the animal, the impulse of self-preservation. To live in harmony with nature is to live reasonably, according to the Stoics. Rational activity is virtue and happiness. Happiness consists exclusively in virtue; the good and the useful coincide with duty and reason. The thought that in moral activity I recognize myself as a conscious intelligence obeying the divine intelligence of the universe exalts human personality to its supremest height. The human will is deified in its identification with universal law through self-conscious obedience.

The activity of man is directed to the individual, the particular; but to make these its final aim is to contradict its divine nature. The individual and the particular must be subordinated to the universal; appetite and emotion must be subordinated to reason. It is the glory of the Stoics, the source of their moral energy and austerity, that they hold so strictly to the universal; that they define it abstractly is a defect and shortcoming. There is a sense in which reason, virtue and happiness are identical; but there is also a sense in which they differ, and this the Stoics disregard.

What is not good in and for itself is not good at all. It may be simply indifferent, something that can be used either for good or evil, as health, riches, honor, life itself. Pleasure is not a good; to make it the aim of life is to turn aside from reason, virtue, and happiness. It is no proof to the contrary that peace of mind follows moral conduct, and inner dissatisfaction its opposite. Pleasure is not the aim, but a result of moral activity, different from virtue in essence and kind. "We do not love virtue because it gives us pleasure," says Seneca, "but it gives us pleasure because we love it." And again: "In doing good man should be like the vine which has produced grapes, and asks for nothing more. . . . . To ask to be paid for virtue is as if the eye demanded a recompense for seeing, or the feet for walking." Pleasure in its very nature is perishable; virtue is enduring and eternal. Pleasure is dependent on something external to itself; virtue is independent, its reward lies in its own nature, it possesses in itself every condition of happiness. But happiness with the Stoics is negative in so far as it is freedom from disturbance, mental tranquillity rather than positive enjoyment.

Grounded in the universal order of the world, virtue opposes man as law, but as the law of his own being and its final cause. Obedience to law is imposed upon him by his own inmost self. His recognition of the reason within him is his recognition of moral responsibility. The good alone is worth striving for, it is that to which he naturally aspires. Were he purely rational no struggle would be required for its achievement. But he is not, he possesses emotions and passions contrary to nature and reason. Their source is false opinion. From an irrational view of what is good arise pleasure and desire, one referring to the present, the other to the future; in the same way care and fear spring from an irrational view of what is evil. True virtue consists in their complete subjugation and suppression. The wise man will be free from pleasure and pain, from desire and fear; he will feel no joy, no suffering, no pity. Virtue as this negative ideal is apathy rather than rational activity; the universal is seized abstractly and contradicts itself. The emotional life of man belongs to the side of his separate existence; to ignore it is to lose sight of his humanity.

But for all its abstractness the grandeur of the Stoic principle is not to be disputed. Stoicism was a system of discipline, restraining the passions and emotions, dignifying and strengthening the will. Man was to seek and find within himself freedom and independence, in the will to be virtuous. Suffering was no evil because it could not penetrate to this stronghold; even though it might be felt, it could not disturb his inward peace and harmony. This was happiness, a permanent condition of the soul.

As rightly ordered reason, virtue is based upon knowledge. The only guide to virtue is knowledge; the only aim of knowledge is rational action. Neither can be conceived without the other. Virtue can be taught, but it can never be attained by mere exercise or habit. It lies wholly in the intention; the will to perform a good action is worth as much as its execution. An evil desire is evil though it may not be gratified. Virtue does not admit of degrees; we have it wholly, or not at all. "In order to drown it is not necessary to be five hundred leagues under water; an ell is sufficient."

Who, then is virtuous? The ideal wise man, say the

Stoics, landing us in another paradoxical abstraction; the rest of the world are fools. The wise man is absolutely good; he who lacks wisdom is absolutely evil. To pass from folly to wisdom is instantaneous conversion.

Practically, the Stoics were obliged to deviate from this rigid ideal in the direction of the ordinary view of life, admitting relative as well as absolute good. But as expressing their philosophy, it has a peculiar significance. Hegel explains it as the will of the subject that wills itself only as the good because it is good, wills its own freedom, and as the inner consciousness withdrawn into itself is wholly separated from and unmoved by the external. It is a personal ideal because virtue to the Stoics consists in the preservation and maintenance of self-consciousness as reason. The one is defined by the other, and there is no way out of the circle. "The goodness of man lies in devotion to the ideal of humanity," says Prof. T. H. Green, "and the ideal of humanity consists in the goodness of man."

Virtue is the moral essence of the individual, but of the individual conscious of self as universal reason. This is the truth of Stoic morality. Self-consciousness reaches the negative moment of abstraction from real existence, comprehending its own essence as reason and therefore freedom, giving up everything but preserving itself in this surrender by making it voluntary—an act of self-conscious intelligence. The subjective becomes the objective, but the Stoics comprehend the two merely as self-identity, not as self-distinction and self-determination in a concrete world of real existence. The ideal wise man is released from every sensuous limitation; "he is free even in fetters, for he acts from himself, unmoved by fear or desire." "He alone is king, for he owes allegiance to no one but himself, and is not bound by the laws." Whatever he does is virtuous. From this point of view the basest action might be justified. But the deeper insight would be that such an action is impossible to the wise man, who is and must remain ideal.

That the ideal is duty for its own sake, a categorical imperative, the Stoics, like Kant, emphasize. But they do not show that it is a process of realization in human society and human conduct, reaching upward continually to an ever higher summit of self-realization and self-perfection. Man is conscious of himself as the final end of his own action, but he is also conscious of himself as a progressive being, passing from possibility to realization, and again to possibility. Otherwise morality would be impossible.

We can reach no higher ideal than the Stoic, that virtue is genuine only when resting on a pure will, the will to do good, directed not to anything external, but to its own perfection. Its negative aspect is its complete renunciation of the sensuous and the emotional in human life, whose relative worth they admit, practically requiring only their subordination to reason. Individual man is to seek for himself moral independence in the development and perfection of his own inner being, recognizing himself as reason, which he does not possess exclusively, but shares with all men. On one hand, he is required to live for the common good and for society; on the other, he is required to live for himself only in the inward consciousness of virtue. He is led by the first to seek companionship; by the second, to dispense with it wholly. The first culminates in citizenship of the world; the second in the self-sufficingness of the wise man. Virtue is the surrender of the individual to the whole, obedience to the common law; but it is also the harmony of man with himself, the rule of his higher nature over the lower, elevation above everything which does not belong to his true being.

Individual self-culture and the social well-being of the community are not elements which oppose each other absolutely, they are rather parts of one great whole. Man must live for his fellow-men, or he cannot truly live for himself. "The whole universe which you see around you, comprising all things, both divine and human, is one. We are members of one great body. Nature has made us relatives when it begat us from the same materials and for the same destinies. She planted in us a mutual love, and fitted us for a social life." Human virtue culminates in social virtue, justice; to love other men is to be more truly natural than to love one's self. We must at the same time love and be just to our fellow men. Justice does not exclude beneficence, benevolence, a readiness to forgive. "Men were born for the sake of men, that each should assist the others." "Nature has inclined us to love men, and this is the foundation of the law."

The action of the wise man benefits all other men; to lift a finger reasonably is to serve the whole world.

The wise man alone knows how to love rightly, because he alone loves not for external advantage, but for inner worth. Genuine friendship is a fraternal union of the wise and the good; its value is in itself alone. Seneca tells us that we must love our friend not because he can help and cherish us, but as one whom we can help and cherish, and for whom, if need be, we can suffer and die.

Man as man, a citizen not of the state but of the world, is the object of interest with the Stoics; politics is subordinated to ethics. We are no more related to one than to another; we are all limbs of one body, or, according to Epictetus, we are all brethren and children of one father. The moral consciousness is here widened to universality; withdrawn into his own interior being, man recognizes its spiritual essence as universal, the divine in all men. The Stoics proclaim with energy a universal human brotherhood.

Man's ethical relation to the world is predetermined by destiny, the law of the universe, to which he must submit unconditionally. This dogma springs necessarily from the Stoic point of view, but is also the product of an age when Rome like an iron fate dominated the world of external reality. There is only one way to happiness and independence, to will nothing except that which is in the nature of things, and which must therefore be realized. Man must submit his will to the divine will, must yield to destiny; but it is his prerogative as a reasonable being to submit voluntarily. Active resistance is justified only when he is placed in circumstances that force him to unworthy conduct. Suicide is the highest expression of moral freedom. Life in itself is not regarded as good, nor death in itself as evil; they are only so relatively. "A philosopher should never commit suicide," says Seneca, "in order to escape suffering, but only to withdraw from restraints in following out the aim of his life."

The moral theory of the Stoics begins with the recognition of the divine as reason controlling the activity of man; it ends with the requirement that man shall submit his will to the will of God. Moral duty springs from a basis of religion, from the common relation of all men to God. Stoicism, like Platonism, is in part a religious system as well as a philosophy. Whatever harmonized with his thought in the popular faith the Stoic accepted, but without criticism. The old myths were interpreted anew. A natural connection was seen between the oracle and the gift of prophecy. This gift rests on the relationship between God and the human soul; purity of heart is its essential condition. The spirit of man, wholly withdrawn from the sensuous and external, is open to the revelation of the spirit of God.

Stoicism expresses the character of an age that cared little for scientific research or the joy resulting from practical action. But it was an age that in the overthrow of states recognized more fully the idea of humanity. Man was to become free and happy through the reasonable exercise of will. But he was regarded only as the organ of universal law, which he must obey. The common moral obligation was recognized, but not the right of the individual to act conformably to his own peculiar character. The part was depressed that the whole might be exalted as universal humanity.

"The Stoic principle is a necessary moment in the idea of absolute consciousness," says Hegel; "it is also a necessary appearance of the time. For if, as in the Roman world, the life of real spirit was lost in the abstract universal, so must the consciousness whose universality is destroyed go back into its individuality to maintain itself in thought." Right and morality were disappearing from the common life of men; consciousness was thus led to maintain their subjective existence as its own inner freedom, giving up all relation to the outer world. The Stoics did not reach the higher insight which would make the outer the realization of the inner, expressing subjective freedom objectively in laws and institutions. Self-consciousness of their universal validity is the harmony between the reasonable will and reality. On one side, the objective system of freedom exists as external laws and duties that I must obey; on the other, obedience is freedom when I recognize their source in myself as reason constituting their reality and my own. The Stoics made the inner freedom of self-consciousness the basis of morality, but did not develop its concrete form wherein the two antithetical sides, the external world and the internal conscience, annul and complete each other in one harmonious whole.

CHAPTER XXXII.

EPICUREANISM.

SIDE by side with the Stoic school of philosophy flourished its adversary, the Epicurean. Epicurus was born 342 B. C. Little is known of him until in his thirty-sixth year he began to teach philosophy in Athens. The seat of his school was his garden; its spiritual centre was his own personality. Never did teacher inspire more love and veneration. His disciples were devoted friends who lived with him in a permanent social union, bound by ties of affection so strong that Epicurus refused to permit a community of goods, saying that it would indicate mistrust, and that friends should confide in one another. That he was worthy of the love and esteem which he inspired, his contemporaries testify.

After his death, which took place in his seventy-first year, he was so deeply honored and revered that no one ever ventured to make a single change in his system of thought. His maxims and doctrines were committed to memory; philosophy to the Epicureans was a body of mechanical tradition rather than a living process of development. The ground of this is found in the system itself, whose only activity is the negation of thought by thought.

Epicurus was a voluminous writer, surpassing even

the Stoic Chrysippus in the number of his works. Most of them are lost, but among those which are preerved are the summaries of his system, which he himself composed. Among his disciples none were more famous than the Roman poet Lucretius, who has embodied in didactic verse the Epicurean doctrines. Other sources of information are Diogenes Laertius, Sextus Epicurus, and the Stoic Seneca.

The aim of philosophy, according to Epicurus, is to promote happiness by means of thought and speech. He goes to the extreme in subordinating theoretical to practical interests; all knowledge is useless that does not minister to practical need. Nature is to be studied, not for itself, but to free the soul from the terror of superstition. So, too, with human instinct and desire. They are to be investigated only that we may control and limit them to natural need. Philosophy is divided into canonics, or logic, physics, and ethics; but the first two exist for the third, to which they are wholly subordinated.

LOGIC.

Epicurus referred everything to the feeling of pleasure or pain; the test of truth is sensuous perception. His point of view is that of common life: what I see, hear, feel, experience through the senses, is real. Sensation is always to be trusted; a delusion of the senses is a mistake of judgment. Error lies not in sensation, but in opinion. Sensuous perception is itself clear evidence. Through its repetition a general picture of what has been perceived is retained by the mind. This is the concept, or notion, which, like perception, is true in itself, needing no proof. The two are the necessary presupposition and criterion of knowledge. We must admit their validity in order to escape universal doubt. The aim of logical inquiry is simply to establish a test of truth.

PHYSICS.

In natural science Epicurus followed Democritus as the Stoics followed Heraclitus. He places the end of action in each individual taken by itself, and what is so absolutely individual as atoms? Nothing exists except atoms and empty space; there is no third, as mind or intelligence. The atoms have weight as well as shape and size, and are moved by natural necessity. But they have also the smallest degree possible of self-motion, and as they fall are able to swerve aside slightly from the perpendicular line, the strict law of gravity. Upon this curious doctrine rests the freedom which Epicurus attributes to the human will. There is no design in nature; its appearance is merely an accidental result of material causes. We see because we have eyes, but we do not possess eyes in order to see.

The human soul is composed of the lightest and most easily moved atoms; this is evident from the speed of thought. The soul consists of two parts, the rational and irrational. The rational has its seat in the breast; the irrational is diffused through the body as a principle of life. This is but another way of distinguishing between mind and matter, according to Zeller. The soul dies with the body; the time when we shall no longer exist affects us as little as the time before we existed.

Hegel says that Epicurus may be regarded as the inventor of empirical natural science and empirical psychology. He made analogy the principle of explanation, reasoning from the known to the unknown; he opposed efficient to final cause; experience to him was sensuous reality. All this was developed superficially, but its result as a knowledge of natural causes tended to free men from belief in omens, divination, and superstitious rites generally. Epicurus, like the modern scientist, argued that the explanation of the natural would banish all fear of the supernatural. He criticized the gods of the popular faith, but believed in their eternal existence and happiness, withdrawing from them only what was unfitting to their divinity.

ETHICS.

The study of physics is intended to overcome the prejudices that stand in the way of happiness; the study of ethics explains the nature of happiness and the means for its attainment. The only unconditional good, according to Epicurus, is pleasure, which may result from motion or from rest; the only unconditional evil is pain. This conviction is presupposed in all our activity; from the first moment of existence the living being seeks pleasure and avoids pain.

But there is a difference of degree in pleasure and pain; we must consider their relation one to the other, must renounce pleasure to escape greater pain, and endure pain to attain greater pleasure. In order to compare and choose between the two intelligence is necessary, insight into their real nature. The state of the mind is more important than the state of the body. Sensuous enjoyment is but for a moment and contains much that is disturbing; mental enjoyment is pure and lasting. So, too, bodily pain is less severe than mental suffering, which stretches over the past and the future as well as the present. The only distinction that Epicurus makes between the mental and the physical, is the addition of memory or hope or fear to the present feeling of pleasure or pain. The supreme good is not to suffer; for the body no pain, for the soul no trouble.

How are we to attain the tranquillity that nothing can disturb? Through free choice. Though the soul is but an assemblage of atoms it has the power of deviating from its natural inclination. This power intelligently directed enables man to evade the law of destiny, to break through the chain of causes and effects, to free himself from outward and inward necessity. The superior is derived from the inferior; the origin of freedom is found in the physical, and not in the nature of divine activity, as with Aristotle.

Epicurus bases his moral theory on pleasure, but pleasure arising from the exercise of virtue. The two are identified, but in a manner opposed to that of the Stoics; virtue is never an end in itself, it is simply the means to an external aim, pleasure. The source of pleasure is not the consciousness of duty fulfilled, or virtuous activity itself; it is freedom from fear, danger, and all that disquiets the soul. A wise self-control will teach us how to enjoy the most and suffer the least. But, with an inconsistency that attracts us and leads us to believe in the genuine unselfishness of human nature, Epicurus insists that we must do good, not from compulsion, nor from regard to others, but from joy in the good itself; that we must obey not the letter, but the spirit of the law.

Real wealth consists in limiting our wants; not to *use* little, but to *need* little, is the true source of self-satisfaction. The Epicurean wise man, unlike the Stoic, is not wholly free from desire and emotion, but through moderate self-restraint prevents their exercising an injurious influence over his life. He is neither a cynic nor a beggar. But Epicurus asserts that he will be happy under all circumstances, and this is the paradox of the Stoics, which seeks to make man free in himself as infinite thought or self-consciousness independent of everything external.

Epicurus ascribes little worth to the state and civil society. He asserts that they are organized merely for an external purpose, mutual safety and protection; that justice is binding, not in itself, but for the general good. Political activity, unless for personal security, is regarded as a hindrance to the true aim of life, the attainment of happiness. Zeller thinks it fitting that the soft, timid spirit of the Epicurean should seek the protection of a monarchical form of government, while the stern, unflinching moral teaching of the Stoic should express itself in the unbending republicanism so often encountered in Rome.

The highest form of social life with Epicurus is friendship. This was the logical outcome of his theory of atomism, his view of the individual as a social atom rather than a member of an organic whole. Friendship is a voluntary relation based on individual character and inclination, unlike that of the state which does not admit of personal choice It is to be cultivated on account of its utility, but it is also maintained that it exists for itself in so far as self-love and the love of a friend are equally strong. We need the help and approval of those whom we love to give firmness to conviction, to rise above the changing circumstances of life. The aim of friendship is the self-enjoyment of cultivated personality. It is the highest earthly good; the wise man will even die for his friend if necessary. Friendship was not only taught but practiced by the Epicureans, with a depth and ardor of sentiment characteristic of a philosophy based on feeling rather than on thought.

The Epicurean ethics reflect the gentle, humane spirit of their founder. Epicurus insisted on compassion and forgiveness, and even declared that it is better to give than to receive. If he did harm by his theory of the utility of virtue, he at the same time taught men that true happiness is mental serenity, and can only be attained through self-culture and self-development. If he made pleasure the end of action, it was pleasure watched over and weighed by understanding and reflection, the result of thought rather than of feeling. His ethical principle seems to culminate in selfishness and egotism, and is diametrically opposed to the Stoic; yet both aim towards inner independence of everything external, an ideal freedom of self-consciousness. The Stoic cannot separate happiness from virtue; the Epicurean cannot separate virtue from happiness.

Both agree that passion must be held in check by reason; but with the Epicurean the restraint is from a prudential motive; with the Stoic the restraint is itself virtue. Both presuppose as the basis of their thought subjectivity limited to itself, expressed in their highest aim as the ideal wise man, self-sufficient in solitude.

It is one and the same principle which we view from opposite sides, in Stoicism and Epicureanism, says Zeller, the principle of abstract self-consciousness developed to universality. To produce this self-consciousness is the aim of philosophy. The Stoic seeks to realize it by subordinating the individual to the universal law; the Epicurean, by freeing the individual from dependence on anything external. The subject is conceived by the Stoic as thought, by the Epicurean as feeling. To one the highest good is therefore virtue; to the other, pleasure. But pleasure regarded as a whole, and conditioned through insight and the action corresponding to insight, is not unlike virtue in its result. Happiness, to the Epicurean as to the Stoic, is an inward harmony of the soul.

Both Epicureanism and Stoicism turn from metaphysics to ethics, from Plato and Aristotle to Socrates and the Socratic schools. Yet both look for independence of the senses in self-consciousness, in subjective activity, which is a one-sided application of the idealism of Plato and Aristotle. Both express a certain stage in the development of Greek thought, a necessary one in philosophy, according to Hegel.

The abstract universality of thought is the principle of the Stoics; the abstract universality of feeling is the principle of the Epicureans. Both argue that knowledge must be possible, or there could be no certainty of action. But Scepticism annuls their one-sidedness and carries to the extreme the withdrawal of man into himself, renouncing all claim to knowledge and all interest in the external world. Subjectivity reaches complete abstraction; scepticism is a negative that remains negative and knows not how to transform itself into something affirmative.

CHAPTER XXXIII.

SCEPTICISM.

PHILOSOPHY, according to Hegel, contains in itself the negative of scepticism as its own dialectic, a negative that becomes affirmative in the living process of knowledge. The seed is negated, destroyed, yet re-affirmed in the plant. The negative is not the final, but a necessary element of concrete reality. Scepticism regards it as the contradictory appearance, a negative that destroys the possibility of knowledge. Neither the Stoic nor the Epicurean principle are valid; we cannot prove the existence of virtue or pleasure, the truth of reason or of the senses, the physics of pantheism or of atomism. Everything wavers amid universal uncertainty except abstract personality content with itself.

Three schools appeared in succession, the Old Scepticism, the New Academy, and the Later Scepticism. The last was in part a revival of the first, but the New Academy was distinct from both, not only because it claimed to follow the teachings of Plato, but as directed principally against the dogmatism of the Stoics, and less radical in its sceptical doctrines than the other schools.

The most eminent leaders of the New Academy were its founder, Arcesilaus, and his successor, Carneades. Arcesilaus affirmed that the subjective conviction of self-consciousness is not a criterion of truth; that we cannot attain knowledge, and must therefore be guided by probability. The connection of this principle with the dialectic of Plato, regarded negatively, or the Ideas as abstract Universals, is apparent.

In his polemic against the Stoics Arcesilaus argued that their principle is contradictory, in so far as it is thought thinking something other than itself. This is the same distinction expressed in modern philosophy as the contrast between thought and being, ideality and reality, subjective and objective. How can I, the internal thinking subject, know the external object?

Knowledge to Arcesilaus is incomprehensible; we can only attain to probability through culture and understanding. Probability is a practical guide, enabling us to choose the good and avoid the evil; it is the basis of virtue.

A century later, Carneades developed more completely the negative and the positive side in the teaching of Arcesilaus. On a foundation of absolute doubt he built the certainty of practical conduct. Truth is unattainable, but a conviction resting on its *appearance*, probability, is indispensable for practical activity. There are three degrees of probability: the first and weakest is a representation which produces alone and for itself the impression of truth; a higher degree is the confirmation of this impression by all the other representations which are connected with the first; the highest of all is a thorough investigation of their relation, which produces perfect conviction.

The Academic principle is not truth, but subjective

certainty. As probability, it is a positive principle, the basis of moral activity. Its scepticism is not so complete and thorough-going as that of the other schools, which precede, accompany, and follow its own.

Pyrrho of Elis, a contemporary of Aristotle, is regarded as the head of the old Sceptics. He left no writings; what we know of his thoughts is derived from Timon of Phlius, his disciple. It is probable that his doctrines are sometimes confused with those of his followers.

Scepticism, like Stoicism and Epicureanism, is practical in its tendency; the aim of philosophy is happiness. To be happy we must understand how things are and how we are related to them; what we can know and what we are to do. They *appear* so and so, but we can never say what they *are*. There is nothing concerning which men agree; the testimony of reason and of the senses is contradictory; one and the same thing can be affirmed or denied. We must therefore suspend judgment and regard everything as undecided, even indecision itself. Our mental attitude must be one of sceptical indifference. We cannot make a positive assertion; we can only say "it is possible," "perhaps," or, if we are very cautious, "I assert nothing, not even that I assert nothing."

From the renunciation of positive conviction, the certainty that we can know nothing, will result imperturbability of spirit, mental equanimity, the withdrawal into inner self-consciousness, which is the ideal happiness of the Sceptic as of the Stoic and the Epicurean. He who who holds that things in their nature are good or evil, is always restless either because he does not possess the good or fears the evil. But he who is sceptical as to their existence neither seeks the one nor flees the other, but remains mentally firm and undisturbed. The wise man is free from opinion, from prejudice, from desire, from emotion; he is indifferent to sickness and health, life and death; he is, in fact, divested of humanity. This is the abstract ideal of Scepticism, but in so far as it is unattainable in ordinary life the Sceptic will follow tradition and probability.

The various ways in which reason and feeling contradict themselves, justifying doubt, were set forth by the Sceptics in ten tropes, collected by Ænesidemus, who lived after Cicero. The first is based on the difference existing in the animal organism which results in difference of feeling and perception, as for instance, when one sees green where another sees yellow. The second trope deals with the differences found among men. Men are unlike one another mentally as well as bodily. They differ in taste, in philosophy, in religion. The greatest minds of the ages do not agree; Heraclitus opposes the Atomists, Aristotle opposes Plato, the Stoics the Epicureans, etc. It would be presumption to attempt the certainty which they could not reach. Inactivity of reason is therefore virtue.

Hereupon Hegel remarks that some people see everything in a system of philosophy except philosophy itself. The different systems of thought, though relatively opposed, really complete one another in so far as the fixed principle in each becomes an organic element of the whole. Truth is essentially a living process, and cannot be limited to one system or expressed in it completely.

The third trope relates to the different functions of the organs of sense. The ear cannot perceive color, nor the eye sound; how, then, can they agree regarding any object? The fourth trope notes the different circumstances under which objects appear to the same subject, when he is asleep or awake, drunk or sober, young or old, etc. Everything *appears*, but nothing *is*. The fifth trope relates to the diversities of appearances due to position, distance, and place. One and the same thing seems large or small, according to its distance from the observer. So, too, it appears different in a different position or place. The sixth trope is derived from intermixture, the fact that no single thing is isolated, but is mixed with other things, so that we never see pure light, or hear pure sound. The testimony of sensation is therefore obscure and untrustworthy. The seventh trope relates to the quantity and modification of the objects of perception. For instance, glass is transparent, but loses this peculiarity if subjected to pressure; or, a little medicine may be beneficial, but a great deal would be fatal.

The eighth trope is general relativity, the substance of all other sceptical tropes, according to Sextus Empiricus. Since everything is only in relation to something else we can know nothing of its real nature. The ninth trope relates to the frequent or rare occurrence of a thing which affects our judgment concerning its worth. The tenth trope is ethical, and treats of the diversities of opinion, culture, customs, laws, myths and scientific theories, which make it impossible for us to judge what is right or wrong. If there is only a subjective test for knowledge, it will go over into scepticism, when its ground is thoughtfully investigated.

All the tropes are directed against the dogmatism of human understanding, which says, "This is so, because I find it so in my experience." It is easy to see that from a different point of view the opposite can be affirmed as equally valid. To find a feeling in myself is not a proof of its existence in another; I can assert that it *appears*, but not that it *is*, because to him it is *not*.

Hegel mentions five other tropes, supposed to have been collected by Agrippa, that belonged to a higher culture of philosophic thinking than the preceding. The first is difference of philosophic opinions; the second is infinite progress; the third is relativity of determinations; the fourth is presuppositions, or setting out from some proof illegitimately assumed; the fifth is proof in a circle where that on which the proof rests must itself be established by that which is proved. They are all contradictions into which understanding falls, and are directed against dogmatic philosophy, not in the sense that it has a positive content, but that it affirms something limited as an absolute. The consciousness of the negative and the definition of its forms found in Scepticism, is of the highest importance in philosophy.

The doctrines of Pyrrho sank into obscurity for a time, but were revived by the later Sceptics, Ænesidemus, Agrippa, Sextus Empiricus, and others. To the works of the Greek physician Sextus, called Empiricus because he belonged to the empiric sect, we are greatly indebted for our knowledge of the doctrines of Scepticism.

CHAPTER XXXIV.

ECLECTICISM.

"SCEPTICISM forms the bridge from the one-sided dogmatism of the Stoic and Epicurean philosophy to Eclecticism," says Zeller. Though it marks a decline of philosophic originality it presupposes a standard given in subjective consciousness which enables one to apprehend the true and reject the false. In the highest sense of the word it seeks to unite concretely the abstract one-sided principles of different systems of thought.

An external influence toward Eclecticism was the study of Greek philosophy in Rome. Rome wished to make the whole world one Roman nation, to unite in one system all philosophy, measuring its value by the test which she applied to everything, practical utility. Cicero is the chief representative of Roman Eclecticism. But he is rather an interpreter of Greek philosophy to his countrymen than an independent investigator. His own basis is doubt; we can not attain positive certainty, but as much as we need for practical life. The consciousness of right is implanted in us by nature and is immediate knowledge. So, too, with the consciousness of God, the freedom of the will, and the immortality of the soul; they are inwardly attested and need no other proof.

The writings of the great Roman Stoics, Seneca, Epictetus, and Marcus Aurelius, deviate slightly toward Eclecticism; the principle of Stoicism through firmly held approaches more and more the principle of universal human love. The aim of philosophy is not only inner freedom and independence, as in older Stoicism, but healing and consolation.

Seneca dwells upon human weakness and the need of help. He exhorts us to be clement and merciful, to spare rather than punish. He directs us to strict self-examination that we may recognize and overcome error and imperfection.

To Epictetus the philosopher is a physician who helps those whom he teaches by awakening the desire for spiritual improvement. The beginning and end of wisdom is to know what is and is not in our power. The first is the sphere of activity; the second is that of submission. Nothing but the will to be good depends on us solely; fate can not touch us if our only striving is toward moral perfection. Epictetus is less proud and more loving than the older Stoics; he extends brotherly sympathy and forbearance to all men, even the most erring and wretched.

A spirit even more humane and gentle pervades the *Meditations* of Marcus Aurelius. "There is but one thing of real value," he writes; "to cultivate truth and justice, and to live without anger in the midst of lying and unjust men." The soul can find repose only in itself; reason is the citadel to which man must flee if he would be invincible. Reason is in all men; the erring, err involuntarily, because they do not recognize their true interest. He who commits injustice injures himself more than others; we can only pity the base and the weak.

The character of Marcus Aurelius was almost perfect. "Seldom indeed has such active and unrelaxing virtue been united with so little enthusiasm," says Lecky, "and been cheered by so little illusion of success." "Never hope to realize Plato's Republic," he writes. "Let it be sufficient that you have in some slight degree ameliorated the condition of mankind, and do not think that amelioration of small importance."

One of the adherents of Eclecticism in Greece was the celebrated biographer, Plutarch. To create moral character was his aim in philosophy. He believed, with Aristotle, that practice, the cultivation of the habit of virtue, precedes actual virtue. One must not, like the Stoic, root out passion and affection, but moderate and guide them; they are the matter of virtue, reason is its form. We can not control external circumstances, but we can use them as a moral help or hindrance. There is no essential difference among men except that of virtue and vice. Religion is the culmination of ethics. There are not different gods for different nations, but One Reason rules the world, named and worshiped differently according as the holy symbols which guide the human spirit to the Divine are more obscure or more distinct.

Plutarch is classed with the Neo-Pythagoreans, among the precursors of Neo-Platonism. The same tendency appears in the Alexandrian School, especially in Philo, who unites Hebraic theology with Hellenic philosophy. His moral theory resembles the Stoic, but lacks its support in self-consciousness, which according to Philo is sinful. The aim of philosophy is the moral salvation of men; its first problem is self-knowledge. The deeper we penetrate within, the greater is our distrust of self. We can attain wisdom only through self-renunciation, complete surrender to God. Philosophy culminates in the absolute absorption of self in the Divine self, immediate union with Deity.

CHAPTER XXXV.

NEO-PLATONISM.

GREEK philosophy closes in Neo-Platonism, a final attempt to solve all its problems, not by setting up a new principle, but by restoring and interpreting Platonism in the sense and according to the spirit of the age, an age that cared more for subjective than objective reality. The longing after a higher mediation of truth than man finds in himself, is the root of Neo-Platonism. Intuition of Deity attained through self-intuition, is its ruling centre. The aim of philosophy is placed in that which transcends reason, immediate unity with God. Its problem is to derive everything finite from Deity—yet separate Deity absolutely from the finite. To bridge the chasm between God and the world requires mediation, degrees of ascent and descent. Man stands on the limit of the sensuous and the super-sensuous; he must elevate himself through self-activity out of the one into the other. In its theory of the transcendence of Deity and a graded transition from the infinite to the finite, Neo-Platonism resembles Oriental philosophy; but the foreign material from whatever source obtained is so blended and transformed as to constitute an integral part of its own system.

PLOTINUS.

The most important representative of Neo-Platonism is Plotinus. He was born in Egypt in the third century A. D. He studied Platonic philosophy in Alexandria with Ammonius Saccas, a celebrated teacher, who is regarded as the founder of Neo-Platonism. After traveling in Persia and India, Plotinus went to Rome in his fortieth year to lecture on philosophy. He produced a great impression, not only by the extent of his knowledge and the originality of his thought, but by his modesty, his moral earnestness and religious consecration. He was so pure, so inspired, so lifted above worldliness, that even his closest friends approached him with awe and reverence. His writings were collected and published after his death by Porphyry, his disciple and successor.

Plotinus posits as the primitive source of all being that which lies beyond thought, or the world of ideas, the One only. Thought is a duality of subject and object, of essence and activity; the One, therefore, is not thought, but its transcendence. Defined negatively, Primordial Being is that to which we can ascribe no quality, not even reason; defined positively, it is the One, the Good, Absolute Causality. But no concept embraces it, we can say what it is *not*, but not what it *is*, only *that* it is, as the presupposition of thought and being.

From Primordial Being, expressed by Plotinus figuratively as out of its fullness necessarily overflowing, though in itself unmoved and undiminished, the finite proceeds as a stream, contained in but not containing or in any way affecting its source. Primordial Being is the sun which pours through the universe its circle of light, a light that gradually pales as it reaches its limit in the gloom of not-being. The finite is but a shadow of the Infinite.

Zeller characterizes this theory as dynamic pantheism rather than emanation, if by emanation we understand that the Infinite gives any portion of its substance to the finite. This Plotinus denies. But in the progress from the Infinite to the finite and its decreasing perfection, his doctrine is one of emanation. God is not in the many substantially, but dynamically; the divine immanence of things is an effect produced through his causality. The lower is mediated through the higher. What is second or produced cannot be as perfect as the first. The first is nothing but the transcendent Cause; the second, its original effect, is *Nous*, or mind, not thought whose potentiality is separated from its actuality, but thought thinking itself, its own changeless being. This being is not pure unity, but multiplicity in unity. The many are contained in thought as concepts, or Platonic ideas. Ideas are regarded as spiritual forces, mediating the transition from the supersensuous to the sensuous. On one side pure reason comprehends in itself the archetypes of all existence, it is that which moves all forces; on the other the many forces are but one force, the many forms but one form, the many gods but one God.

The product of pure reason is the world-soul, an emanation proceeding eternally from a changeless and undiminished substance, as reason proceeds from Primordial Being. The world-soul mediates between reason and the sensuous appearance, it is the outermost circle of light beyond the central sun; beyond it begin material darkness and nothingness. It differs from reason as the word from the thought, the appearance from the essence. It is the universal soul which contains in itself all individual souls; it is one and indivisible, but each single being receives of it all that it is able to comprehend.

Matter has no reality, it is the mere possibility of being, pure negation. This is Platonic, but Plotinus goes farther, and asserts that matter as privation of good is evil. He regards it as necessary, and traces it to the law which conditions the descent of the imperfect from the perfect, the fading of the illumination from the central light into outermost darkness. The soul at the limit of the supersensuous presses into that which lies outside of itself—matter, out of the eternity of reason into temporal life. It is a fall, a descent, due not to reason, but to its partial obscurity, its withdrawal from Primordial Being towards nothingness.

The sensuous world as a whole is a mere copy of the supersensuous, a mirror of the soul in matter. It is beautiful and perfect as this mirror; the Greek sense of nature is too strong in Plotinus for him to view it as altogether evil and unreal. It is not a house built of dead matter, but a living being, an organic body moved by one soul. Each part is in perfect harmony with the whole, a harmony that is maintained, as in music, by apparent discord and contradiction. Everything is guided by Providence, not as intelligent foreseeing, but as natural necessity, the immanent relation of the sensuous to the supersensuous. The imperfection of the part is necessary for the perfection of the whole; the finite could not be otherwise and remain finite. We have but to coöperate actively with Providence, and that which appears evil is transformed into good.

Lower than the world-soul are the souls of the stars, visible gods who lead a uniform and happy life. Lower yet are are the beings whom Plotinus calls demons, who mediate between the divine and the earthly, who are eternal and supersensuous, yet bound to matter and able to appear at need in bodies of fire or air. The earth, like the stars, is regarded as a thinking being and a god, whose soul overflows into the souls of plants, producing their life and growth. The animal is regarded as either a ray of the world-soul, or a shadowy picture of the human soul bound to an animal body.

The human soul has fallen from the sphere of the supersensuous into that of the sensuous. It was once a part of the world-soul, free from all suffering, outside of time and change, possessing neither remembrance nor self-consciousness because perfectly transparent and absorbed in primal intelligence. But as original unity produces multiplicity, a like necessity compels the soul, standing on the limit of the supersensuous, to illuminate the sensuous. Through experience of darkness its own slumbering forces are awakened, and it realizes for the first time the full glory and perfection of light.

In so far as union with a body springs from the nature and inclination of the soul, it is free activity, but free activity conditioned through universal necessity, the law that rules the whole and subordinates to its perfection the imperfection of the part. The descent of the soul into the sensuous is its inherent weakness, but weakness that can be transformed into strength through its return to the supersensuous. It mediates between the higher and the lower, and thus leads a double existence, its activity directed now to one now to the other. But its peculiar distinction is the higher nature which constitutes the spiritual reality of man, enabling him to apprehend God intuitively, and to live in time as if in eternity, participating in divine intelligence.

The soul cannot suffer, but perceives as a shadowy picture pain and pleasure, which come from the body and the animal principle of life. So, too, the sensuous object cannot affect the soul except through a mediate impression. Memory is the first spiritual activity; but an activity that belongs to the soul as subjected to change and temporal life. It is connected with the faculty of imagination, which has a concealed duality, a higher and a lower function as it reproduces thought or the sensuous image. Consciousness is the reflex of spiritual activity in the faculty of perception; it is mediated through the sensuous, and is therefore not the highest in man. "The act of incarnation is coincident with the attainment of individual consciousness," says Erdmann; "it is freely willed and at the same time punishment,"

Plotinus and the whole Neo-Platonic school maintain that without free-will man could not exist as man, that to be a self-active and independent subject belongs to his essence as a human being. But they do not explain how free-will is to be harmonized with Providence and the necessity that rules the whole, how each creates his own character and yet plays the role in the world-drama assigned to him by the Creator. He who follows his own nature is free because he depends on nothing external to himself; he who strives after the good must act voluntarily. The soul in itself is without error, yet before its entrance into the body freely chose a human life. This is the unsolved contradiction and discord of earthly existence. The true home of the soul is the world of the supersensuous; the body is a prison that it would fain escape. But escape is not through death, only through inward purification.

When the body dies, the soul, according to its will and inner condition, sinks into matter or into vegetative or animal existence, or seeks again a human body or that of a demon, or is raised to the stars and restored to its primal purity and perfection. Plotinus believes in transmigration as the law of eternal justice; the oppressor shall become the oppressed; the master, the slave; the rich, the poor; the murderer, the murdered, etc. But he is not clear as to what constitutes the especial subject of retribution and transmigration, since the soul in itself knows nothing of time or previous existence. It is only what it thinks and as it thinks.

The problem of the soul is to free itself from the body through self-activity. The perfect life is the life of thought, a relation of man to his inner being, independent of everything external. Virtue is not a transformation of character, for the true self is without error, it consists rather in turning away from all that is disturbing. The source of evil is the relation of the soul to the body; purification concerns the relation, and not the soul itself. As the artist needs only to chisel away part of the marble to restore its divine beauty, man needs only to rid himself of the sensuous to restore his soul to its unsullied purity.

Plotinus would not annihilate the sensuous, but subject it to reason. The beauty of the world leads him to a more positive ethical affirmation than is implied in its total renunciation. As a copy of the resplendent Idea it reminds the soul of its heavenly origin, it kindles the desire for the good; the faint earthly reflection helps its ascent toward perfect and absolute beauty. But practical activity is regarded as subordinate to that which is purely theoretic. So far as man works with the external and sensuous he is immersed in the world of appearance, his activity has but a relative value compared with the absolute worth which the soul possesses in itself in thought or theory. Outward activity and representation are good only so far as they lead to spiritual insight and knowledge.

The attention of Plotinus is too exclusively directed

to the inner world of thought for him to pay much attention to the state or the organization of society. Political virtue has its worth in limiting desire and affection; but true wisdom, bravery and justice, are a relation of the soul to itself, not to anything external. The highest interest of man is to live in the world, not as man, but as a god, withdrawn from it entirely in his own inner being, a paradoxical ideal not unlike the Stoic.

Even theoretical activity is imperfect if it rests on sensuous observation and experience. The thinking that is mediated, that separates the knowing subject from the object known, is lower than that which is immediate, blending the two without distinction. The highest knowledge is the self-intuition of reason; withdrawn into its pure essence, human thinking is united with the divine, with the whole of which it is a part. Mystical union with God is the final aim of philosophy. Thought and self-consciousness disappear in a divine ecstasy, absorption in the Absolute One.

Plotinus explains this inward illumination, known to him from his own experience, as the sudden and immediate filling of the soul with the divine light which streams from Deity. It is not knowledge of God, but an ecstatic union of the soul with Primitive Being, a union so perfect as to annul every distinction. The soul is absorbed in the pure light of Deity; there is no part but only the whole. Thought as limitation, self-consciousness as the distinction between subject and object, belong to the finite; the soul exalted to the Infinite is lifted above wisdom and virtue and beauty to a state of religious rapture where it is no longer soul, or self, or thought, but God.

This condition can be attained only through absolute abstraction from the external, the pure absorption of the soul in itself. We are not to seek the inward light but await it quietly; we can not say it comes or goes, but it is here, a sudden illumination of perfect bliss and peace. It is of short duration because the soul bound to a body emerges from this mystical unity into the duality of observer and observed; it descends from the enraptured beholding of God to consciousness of self. This contradiction belongs to its essence as mediating between the higher and the lower, the Infinite and the finite.

Religion is in the closest union with philosophy to Plotinus as to Plato. Plotinus adapts and interprets the myths of the popular faith. He explains prayer through its sympathetic influence as a spiritual force in the universe. Every effect is dynamic rather than physical; the chain of natural causation is magic, sympathetic attraction and repulsion. Prophecy and the belief in enchantment are closely related to magic.

Plotinus could not escape the irresistible tendency of his age, but sought to harmonize its way of thinking with his own deeper insight. He is not so much concerned to explain external reality as to elevate the spirit to the good and the true, and reveal its heavenly origin and destiny.

PORPHYRY.

Plotinus was succeeded by his most distinguished scholar, Porphyry. But in creative force Porphyry is not to be compared with his master. His especial characteristic is the striving towards clearness of thought and expression, so that, as Zeller says, he appears as the most sober and moderate of the Neo-Platonists. He taught both philosophy and eloquence in Rome. He popularized the doctrines of Plotinus, and sought by means of philosophy to purify religious belief and produce true piety. His aim was to heal and console men, to purify and stimulate moral activity. He regarded asceticism as an especial means of purification. He prohibited the eating of flesh not only because it promotes sensuous impulse, but from the fact that animal nature is akin to our own as bodily, and foreign to it as spiritual. Fettered by the body, we are to implore divine help in the struggle towards virtue; religion is indispensable to men who feel their finite weakness. Porphyry subordinates the theological element to the philosophic; the reverse is true of his disciple, Jamblichus.

JAMBLICHUS.

Jamblichus is a theologian rather than a philosopher; what he seeks is the speculative basis of religion. Convinced of the inherent weakness of human nature he declares that it can be purified only through the help of higher beings, of heroes, demons, angels and gods. The soul is free to choose or reject their help, free to turn toward light or darkness, good or evil. We can not know how the gods produce the finite; the first condition of knowledge is faith in their omnipotence. Multiplicity is the character of the supersensuous as of the sensuous; the polytheistic tendency in the philosophy of Jamblichus is not to be mistaken. Historically, it stands on the limit which separates Neo-Platonism as a philosophy from Neo-Platonism as a system of theology.

PROCLUS.

Proclus is the most celebrated of the later Neo-Platonists. He was born in Constantinople 412, A. D. He studied philosophy in Alexandria and Athens. The teacher whom he honored with especial veneration was Syrianus, his immediate predecessor in the Athenian school of Neo-Platonism. When at the death of Syrianus Proclus assumed its leadership, he was already renowned for his learning and piety. So great was the impression he produced that he was revered as an especial favorite of the gods, a model of superhuman moral excellence. He renounced family life to devote himself to knowledge. He was distinguished for a high sense of friendship, unselfish activity, beneficence and humanity.

What he sought in philosophy was nothing less than to unite in one logical whole all the chaotic material of Neo-Platonism, and erect for it a scientific structure. He was especially fitted by speculative genius and religious enthusiasm to grapple with the difficulties of this task. He revered so piously the authority of his predecessors that he wished to be only their interpreter. He united to a wonderful degree the power of abstraction with phantasy, the need of knowledge with faith. He represents Scholasticism in Greek philosophy. His remarkable dialectic insight was fettered by reliance on authority and tradition, and resulted in that unfruitful formalism which, according to Zeller, forms the background of all Scholasticism. His system is the link that mediates the transition from Greek to mediæval philosophy: the close of the one and an anticipation of the other.

His chief striving was to find the law which connects everything as a whole; to explain how the many proceed from and return to the One. Like Plotinus he derived the finite from the Infinite through dynamic causality, but the derivation is a spiral process instead of a simple line. Being as original Cause, as the effect proceeding from and returning to it, are the three moments which eternally represent the process of finite creation. The triune activity that rules the whole is reflected in every part; each sphere of divided being is one in its totality as cause, but proceeds to many effects whose multiplicity can only be annulled by the return to original unity. The threefold relation is thus expressed; the effect in so far as it is like the cause remains in it, in so far as it is unlike the cause separates from it and seeks to become like it, which constitutes the struggle of the finite and its return to the Infinite. Both derivation and return are a spiral descent and ascent, mediated in a triune process through lower or higher spheres of being.

Proclus asserts that the human soul can only rise

above the sensuous to the supersensuous through gradual mediation, which apparently contradicts the fundamental belief of Neo-Platonism that the soul is to seek immediate unity with God. The basis of higher culture is ethical virtue; through it one **must** purify himself and submit to be ruled by reason before he is fit to turn toward the divine. But faith is worth more than knowledge; we cannot in our weakness attain the higher life without divine help. The ways to God are three: love, truth, faith. Love leads us through beauty to truth; truth shows us the world of the supersensuous; faith reveals the highest, the deep mystery of the universe. Not through thinking and reflection, but through that absorption of the soul in itself which we owe to faith, through divine ecstasy and illumination, are we united mystically with God.

This altar of the Absolute One, an ardent and luminous centre in whose divine flame all is consumed and united, is the final aim of the philosophy of Proclus, as of all Neo-Platonism. The soul has only to bury itself in itself to find there the living God. But, closely examined, this religious rapture, this immediate union with Deity, is not feeling, but thought itself in its pure simplicity. It is a higher idealism, but the idealism of thought, an inward illumination that reveals God, but God as the soul of our soul, God as Infinite Reason.

CHAPTER XXXVI.

THE CLOSE OF GREEK PHILOSOPHY.

AFTER the death of Proclus, the Athenian school rapidly declined, and was closed 529 A. D. by an edict of the emperor Justinian. No farther attempt was made by the Greek mind to solve the great problem of the relation between thought and being. Inner exhaustion coincided with external force to bring to a close the magnificent work achieved by human reason in Greek philosophy. It lasted for nine centuries after its quick and glorious bloom in Socrates, Plato, and Aristotle. It was the refuge of the noblest minds in those dark days of political oppression that followed the downfall of Greek independence. It preceded and anticipated in part the teaching of Christianity, but could not accept it wholly without giving up its peculiar character and leaving the ground wherein it was rooted.

Many of the Church Fathers, and some of the ablest modern thinkers, believe that it fulfilled a propædeutic office for Christianity. "Philosophy, before the coming of the Lord, was necessary to the Greeks for righteousness," says Clement; "and it now proved useful for godliness, being in some part a preliminary discipline for those who reap the fruits of faith through demonstration. Perhaps we may say it was given to the Greeks with this special object; for philosophy was to the Greeks what the Law was to the Jews, a schoolmaster to bring them to Christ." "Christianity proceeded along lines of thought that had been laid through ages of preparation," says Dr. B. F. Cocker in " Christianity and Greek Philosophy;" " it clothed itself in forms of speech which had been moulded by centuries of education, and it appropriated to itself a moral and intellectual culture which had been effected by long periods of severest discipline."

History is development of the human spirit according to Divine Law; the present was potentially in the past, the past is actually in the present. To comprehend the thought of to-day we must know the thought of yesterday, and be able to recognize their fundamental unity. Our insight must be deep enough to harmonize what seems discordant and contradictory. The divine is revealed in the constitution and development of the human mind, in the history of its striving after truth and the knowledge of God.

Greek philosophy asserts with overwhelming testimony that the divine is in the human, that the only reality is spirit. It affirms the existence of God and of the soul, and even in its scepticism finds a stronghold which is proof against attack, the infinite subjectivity of human consciousness. In Neo-Platonism, it seeks through mystic exaltation the perfect identification of the Divine and the human; its ideal approaches the ideal of Christianity, the perfect love that loses self to find it in the self of God.

"For thousands of years the same Architect has directed the work," says Hegel, "and that Architect is the one living mind of which the nature is thought and self-consciousness." The content of religion and philosophy is one; faith and knowledge, "God's revelation to man, and man's discovery of God," coincide ultimately.

Greek philosophy manifests the immanence of the divine in human reason; it is the seeking and the finding amid finite error and imperfection of the Infinite. "It was the teacher of the Middle Ages," says Zeller; "the new time began under its guidance; and whenever the independent modern mind needs a fresh stimulus to activity, it goes back gladly to its inexhaustible sources. Our perceptions have widened, our moral and metaphysical concepts have changed, our science has investigated more thoroughly the realm of nature and of spirit, than the Hellenic; but the clearness of glance, the unity of philosophic character, the complete surrender of individuals to their principles, which for the most part characterize the masters of ancient philosophy, will always command admiring wonder and emulation. Regarded as a whole, the history of Greek philosophy, in its uniform and regular development, in the definiteness with which each school comprehends its especial principle, in the purity with which it is worked out, is a source of delight. To hold this great appearance vitally in the consciousness of the present, to nourish the spirit of our time with the fruits of the friendly

Hellenic spirit, is one of the most beautiful and grateful problems of the science of history."

THE END.

www.ingramcontent.com/pod-product-compliance
Lightning Source LLC
Chambersburg PA
CBHW022051230426
43672CB00008B/1134